INTERGALACTIC BASS

SCALES · ARPEGGIOS · FINGERINGS · THEORY & MUCH MORE!

T0057465

BY CARLO MOMBELLI

ISBN 978-1-4768-6889-9

HAL·LEONARD®
CORPORATION
7777 W. BLUEMOUND RD. P.O. BOX 13819 MILWAUKEE, WI 53213

In Australia Contact:
Hal Leonard Australia Pty. Ltd.
4 Lentara Court
Cheltenham, Victoria, 3192 Australia
Email: ausadmin@halleonard.com.au

ACKNOWLEDGEMENTS

First, I would like to thank Andre Steenkamp who introduced me to so much music, and Mrs Loveday and Johnny Fourie who taught me so much music. A big thanks to Rhoda Isaacs-Bopape who introduced me to Reedwaan Vally. Thanks Reedwaan and Angela McClelland for believing in this book from the very first meeting. Thank you to everyone at Real African Publishers and especially Dan Maré, who worked so hard in putting this book together to make it into what it is. I could never have imagined how fine it would look when I first set out on this journey. I would also like to thank Professor Christine Lucia who has shown me that it is still possible to be an artist and be yourself within an academic environment, and to Wits University for the support and opportunities.

I would also like to thank the two music professors, Marc Duby and Mike Campbell, who read through my work, spotted my mistakes and gave me good advice.

A very special thanks to my wife Sandra, who has encouraged and inspired me over the last 28 years to always be the artist I am meant to be. And to my two daughters, Gina and Maria, I thank you for all of your love and inspiration.

Carlo Mombelli
2011 Johannesburg, South Africa

This book is dedicated to
Johnny Fourie

"It is not the number of years you have lived that makes you old. You become old when you stop progressing. As soon as you feel you have done what you had to do, as soon as you think you know what you ought to know, as soon as you want to sit and enjoy the results of your effort, with the feeling you have worked enough in life, then at once you become old and begin to decline. When on the contrary you are convinced that what you know is nothing compared to all that remains to be known, when you feel that what you have done is just the starting point of what remains to be done, when you see the future like an attractive sun shining with innumerable possibilities yet to be achieved, then you are young howsoever many are the years you have passed upon earth – young and rich with all the realizations of tomorrow."

– *Mira Alfasa*

CONTENTS

INTRODUCTION

This book is based on the scale types required to master and understand improvisations in jazz and other styles of music. For the sake of keeping things simple and uncluttered, each page consists of only one scale type, drawn on a bass guitar neck with the correct fingering – a vital part of organising the hands. The more organised the hands, the easier it is to play. It is naturally better to play the bass with as little tension in the hands as possible, so if a certain fingering is less stressful than another that is considered to be technically correct. I believe the bassist must go with the less stressful approach, as one's aim is to play relaxed. Each scale in this book is drawn in open position, 1st position and neck position. On the same page the harmonic structure of the scale appears as well as the chord family and other relevant information such as passing notes, tritones, chord progressions, etc.

As this book is centred around using the correct fingering for the different scale shapes on the bass neck, this technique is better explained using diagrams and not notation. Because it is a good idea to associate finger positions with their notational equivalents, I have also included the notated scale of the neck position shape.

The fingerings shown in these diagrams are from my mental notes of more than 30 years of experimenting and searching as a self-taught bassist. If, however, your hands dictate an easier way of playing these scales and arpeggios, then rather go with that. Because I learnt to play bass on a fretless instrument, these fingerings relate to my fretless bass approach. There are two ways to approach fingering, the 1-2-3-4 shape and the box shape.

The 1-2-3-4 fingering shape

One position = 4 notes, played with the fingering 1-2-3-4, that is one finger per fret. Because the bass is tuned in fourths, the bassist actually needs a fifth finger to play many of the scales vertically. We overcome this small problem by shifting positions a semitone up or down, or, as in the case of the chromatic scale, we add a note outside the position and perform a shift with the 1st finger. The following diagram, showing the chromatic scale, illustrates this.

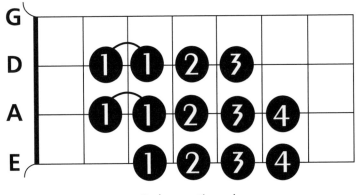

G chromatic scale

Notice that the first finger is the one doing the position shift. In all of the position shifts, especially when playing two-octave scales on a four-string or shifting between modes horizontally, I have found shifting with the 1st or 2nd finger to be the most accurate intonation-wise (on the fretless), and the fastest. In some cases it is necessary to shift with one of the other fingers.

Box Shape fingering

Box shape = three across (horizontally) and three up (vertically), making a box with nine notes in it, and we use the fingering 1-2-4. Therefore, an octave would be played with the 1st and the 4th fingers as illustrated in the following diagram.

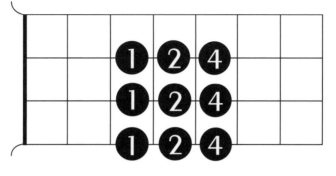

Box shape

A lot of blues lines can be played using this box shape approach.

The natural curve

If the bassist goes to the first position and plays a low F and the octave F simultaneously, his or her hand naturally uses the box shape and falls into the natural curve of the wrist. This results in less tension in the hand and helps fretless players with the optical angle of where the note lies, which helps one stay more in tune.

Moving between 'box shape' and '1-2-3-4', one finger per fret

Sometimes it is necessary to combine both fingering variations. Take a look at the fingering in the next diagram of the white notes played in 1st position on a five-string bass from the low B up to C on the G-string. The scale starts with box shape fingering and converts to 1-2-3-4 finger shape on the G-string.

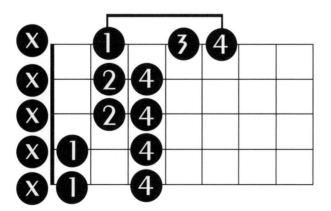

White notes in 1st position (5 string)

Tone – Tone (1-2-4)

When two tones are played on the same string, as in the case of the whole-tone scale, the bassist has to stretch the hand and play using the 1st, 2nd and 4th fingers. This is quite a stretch, but it is easier and more natural to stretch the 1st and the 2nd fingers than the 3rd and the 4th.

Two tones

Open position, first position and neck position shapes

The vertical scales on the bass work with shapes. For example, the shape for a major scale would have the same shape and fingering as another major scale on that same string, so learning the fingering for one shape can be applied to many scales of that same scale type. This is true from the 2nd position going up the neck of the bass. These are the neck position scales. However, scales that start on the 1st fret (the first position), and open strings (the open position), have different shapes even though they are from the same scale type. There is an exception. Some scales on the first and neck position have the same shape, for example the Locrian scale. In these cases the neck position would start on the 1st fret. The fingerings for all three positions are documented in this book.

Three, then Four, then Five

It is just as important to learn a scale using the top three strings of the bass as it is learning a scale on four strings. Therefore all scales in this book are first documented starting on the A string (three strings), and then advancing to four, etc. On three strings the scales go up vertically one octave, but sometimes more if one can still stay in position (shown using a blank circle). On four strings, the vertical scales go up to the 11th, and on a five-string bass the vertical scales can go up two octaves.

The two-octave scale and arpeggio on a four-string bass

There are more than 10 ways of playing a two-octave scale and arpeggio on a four-string bass. Because of the amount of things there are to practice, one usually does not have the time to practice 10 ways of playing the same scale. The bassist must, however, be able to play a two-octave scale using a diagonal shape as well as a shape that goes up vertically then cuts across horizontally on one string. Those scales and arpeggios are also documented in this book.

Finger placement

The bassist must try to place his fingers directly behind the next fret. Not only do we find the best tone at this spot, but the bassist has to create some sort of finger-spacing habit, so that each time he plays, his brain knows that the distance from one note to the next is *x*. By doing this you develop muscle memory in your hand, which is very important, especially for fretless bass players.

Terminology: passing tones

Notes of certain scales are described as passing tones in this book. They may also be described as the 'be careful not to land on' notes, as they generate a dissonance to the harmony. However, it is not absolutely forbidden to land on them, as the musician may want that sound. Therefore the term 'avoid note', which is sometimes used in teaching this aspect, is generally avoided here.

Graphics

The symbol X means 'play open string'.
The symbol ⌐‾‾⌐ means 'one position'.
The symbol ⌒ means 'moving from one position to the next using the same finger'.

The fingerboard dots

I have used black, grey and white dots in this book to indicate various things. On scales where I have indicated the arpeggio, the arpeggio notes are black and the rest are grey.
However, please note that the fingering indicated is the scalar and not the arpeggio fingering and in some cases you will have to adjust your fingering to best suit the different arpeggio leaps.
On Bebop scales the grey dot indicates the extra Bebop note.

Why are blocks included with the music notation in the Jazz Theory section?

In addition to my performance and composition career, I teach at a University where I have, on occasion, had blind students in my class. I changed my jazz notes into blocks for them, which the University then converted into braille. However, many of my other students really understood the theory from these graphics, so I decided to use them in this book so that even non-readers of music notation can understand jazz theory. This must not stop you from learning to read music. It is true that you can speak a language without learning to read or write it, but think of the limitations. You would have no possibility to study from books. Someone else would have to read them to you. You would have no way of documenting your ideas unless, once again, someone else did it for you. Even if you spoke the language well, you would be regarded as illiterate, and to be illiterate puts you at a great disadvantage. The advantages of reading music are endless. So even though I also use graphics in this book to explain the jazz theory, **LEARN TO READ MUSIC.**

Accuracy

Strive for accuracy, not speed, because through accuracy one develops speed, and always practice your scales and arpeggios legato.

Piano friendly

Do yourself a favour and learn where all the notes are on a piano. This will help you to understand music theory a lot better and will also help with your composing.

And finally, a quote from Mark Levin's *Jazz Theory Book*:

> *"Scales are the alphabet, not the poetry, of music. You need to know the alphabet, grammar, vocabulary, spelling, and so on, before you can write words, sentences, and ultimately poetry. The goal is to internalise scale knowledge so completely that scales become an available pool of notes, a pool that you can dip into for any note you want."*

**THE 12 MAJOR SCALES IN 1ST POSITION STARTING ON THE
LOWEST DIATONIC NOTE ON THE LOWEST STRING**

THE CHROMATIC SCALE ON ONE STRING

1.1
12 MAJOR SCALES in 1st position

NOTE: 4 string bass players play the E string as the lowest note. The white dot in this chapter indicates the tonic note of the scale.

C Major

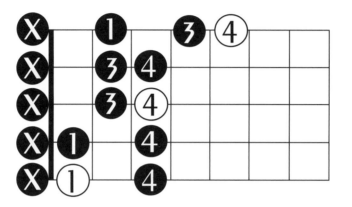

F Major

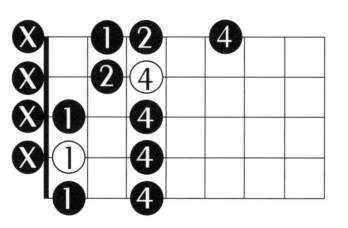

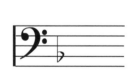

B♭ Major

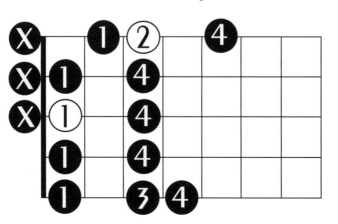

E♭ Major

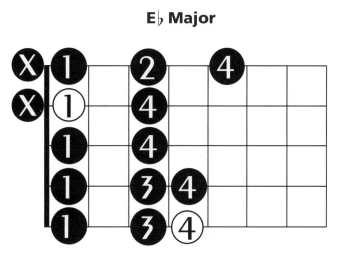

A♭ Major

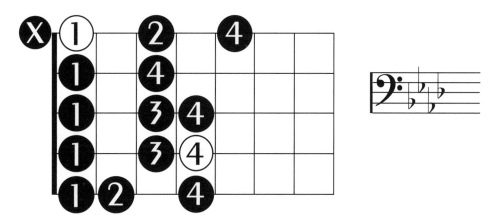

D♭ Major

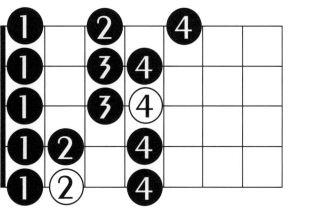

G♭ (F#) Major

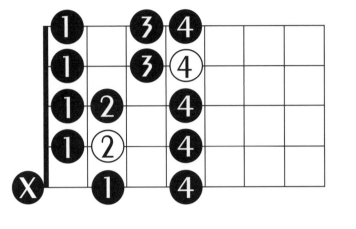

B Major

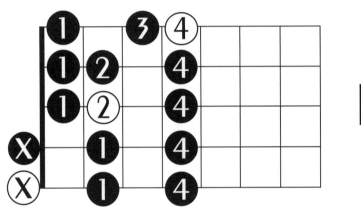

E Major

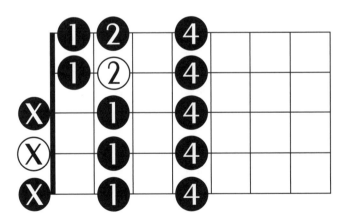

A Major

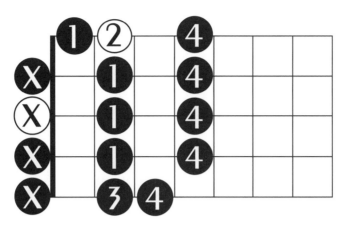

D Major

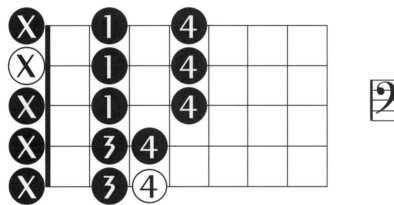

G Major

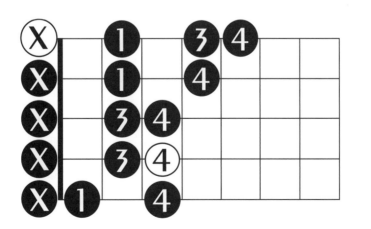

1.2
CHROMATIC SCALE ON ONE STRING – ONE OCTAVE

Open position

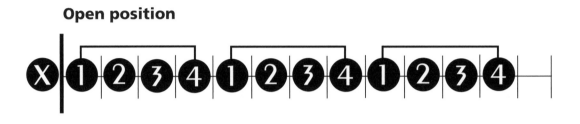

Neck position

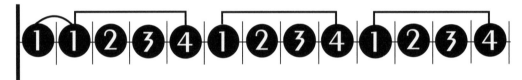

VERTICAL SCALES ON 3 STRINGS

2.1
THE 7 MODES GENERATED BY THE MAJOR SCALE

IONIAN (major) SCALE
mode 1

HARMONIC SPELLING: 1 – 2(9) – 3 – 4 – 5 – 6 – 7 – octave
ARPEGGIO: 1 – 3 – 5 – 7
CHORD FAMILY: Major chords, Maj7, Maj9, Maj6/9
PASSING TONE: 4th

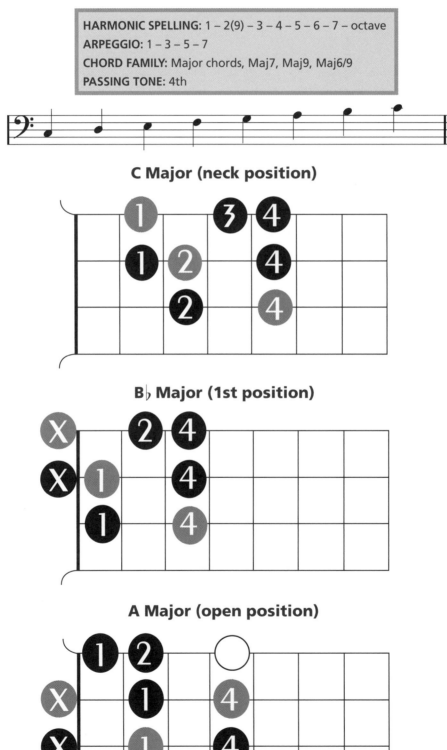

C Major (neck position)

B♭ Major (1st position)

A Major (open position)

DORIAN SCALE
mode 2

HARMONIC SPELLING: 1 – 2(9) – ♭3 – 4(11) – 5 – 6(13) – ♭7 – octave

ARPEGGIO: 1 – ♭3 – 5 – ♭7

CHORD FAMILY: min6, min7, min9, min11, min13.

CHORD PROGRESSION: The Dorian scale is used on minor I chords & the II chord of a II–V–I progression.

SHORTCUT TIP : If we play any Aeolian scale and raise the 6th, we have the Dorian.

C Dorian (neck position)

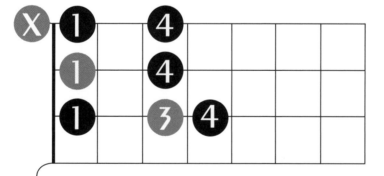

B♭ Dorian (1st position)

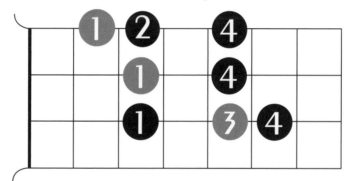

A Dorian (1st position)

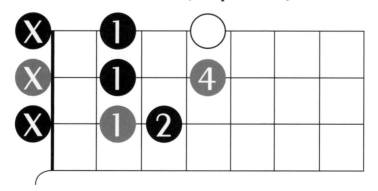

Optional DORIAN SCALE fingering

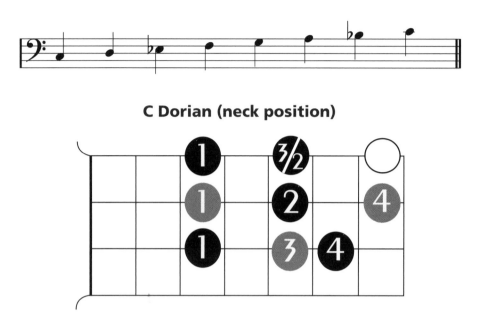

C Dorian (neck position)

PHRYGIAN SCALE
mode 3

HARMONIC SPELLING: 1 – 2(♭9) – ♭3 – 4(11) – 5 – ♭6 (♭13) – ♭7 – octave
ARPEGGIO: 1 – 4 – 5 – ♭7
CHORD FAMILY: sus4♭9
NOTE: Notes most often played on a sus♭9 chord are – root, ♭9, 4, 5, ♭7.
SHORTCUT TIP: Play an Aeolian scale and lower the 2nd note to get a Phrygian scale.

C Phrygian (neck position)

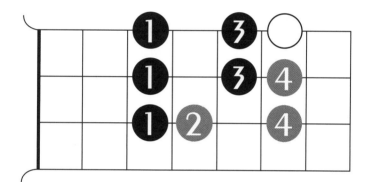

A Phrygian (open position)

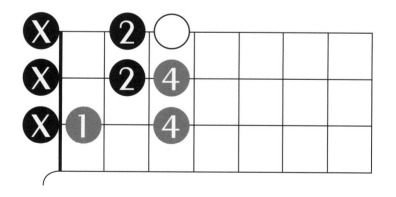

LYDIAN SCALE
mode 4

HARMONIC SPELLING: 1 – 2(9) – 3 – #4(#11) – 5 – 6(13) – 7 – octave
ARPEGGIO: 1 – 3 – 5 – 7
CHORD FAMILY: Maj, Maj7, Maj7♭5, Maj7#11, Maj13#11

C Lydian (neck position)

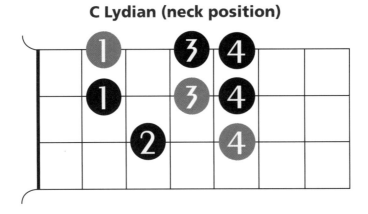

B♭ Lydian (1st position)

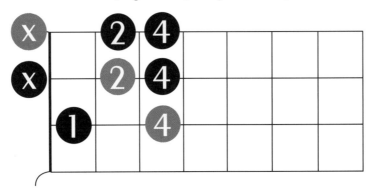

A Lydian (open position)

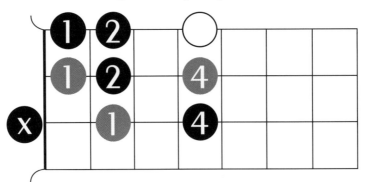

MIXOLYDIAN SCALE
mode 5

HARMONIC SPELLING: 1 – 2(9) – 3 – 4(11) – 5 – 6(13) – ♭7 – octave
ARPEGGIO: 1 – 3 – 5 – ♭7
CHORD FAMILY: Dom7, Dom9, Dom13, 7sus4
PASSING TONE (avoid note) is the 4th (except on a sus4 chord)
CHORD PROGRESSION: Can use the Mixolydian scale on the V7 chord of the II–V–I progression as well as on the Dom7 chords of the blues progression.

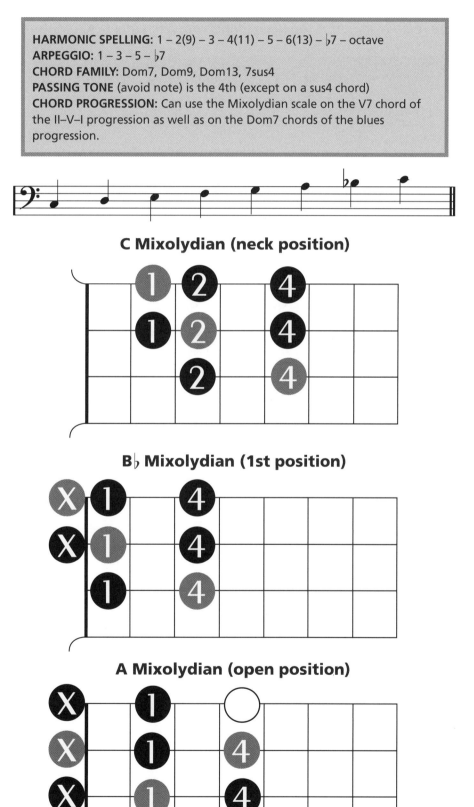

C Mixolydian (neck position)

B♭ Mixolydian (1st position)

A Mixolydian (open position)

AEOLIAN (natural minor) SCALE
mode 6

The relative minor of the major scale with the same key signature.

HARMONIC SPELLING: 1 – 2(9) – ♭3 – 4(11) – 5 – ♭6 – ♭7 – octave
ARPEGGIO: 1 – ♭3 – 5 – ♭7
CHORD FAMILY: min7, min9, min♭6

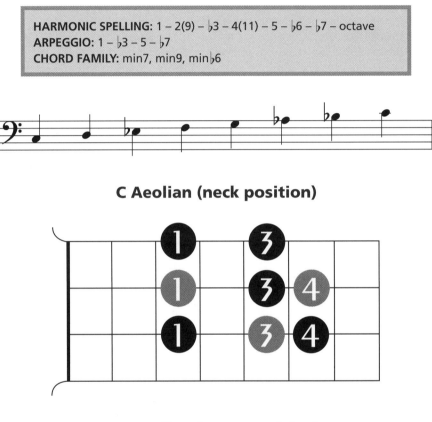

C Aeolian (neck position)

A Aeolian (open position)

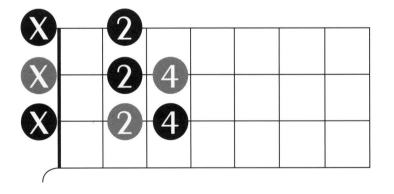

LOCRIAN SCALE
mode 7

> **HARMONIC SPELLING:** 1 – ♭2(♭9) – ♭3 – 4(11) – ♭5 – ♭6 – ♭7 – octave
> **ARPEGGIO:** 1 – ♭3 – ♭5 – ♭7
> **CHORD FAMILY:** min7♭5 or Ø (called a 'half-diminished')
> **PASSING TONE** (avoid note) is the ♭9

C Locrian (neck position)

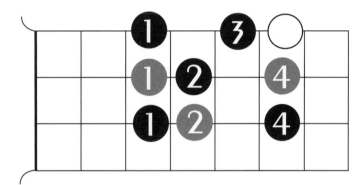

A Locrian (neck position)

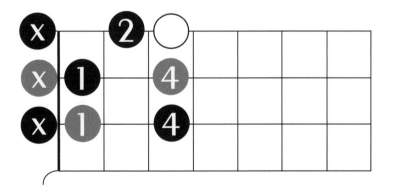

HORIZONTAL SHIFTING BETWEEN THE VERTICAL MODES & 7th ARPEGGIOS

A bassist should be able to shift between the different vertical modes and arpeggios in a horizontal manner. However, when doing this, the fingering of the different modes changes slightly to maintain a smoother feel. Coming down the neck, the fingerings once again change slightly. Because the fingering going up the neck is different to the fingering coming down the neck, both directions have been included in these diagrams.

There are two exercises here.

1. Up / step / down
First we go up on mode 1 then come down on mode 2, then up on mode 3, etc.

2. Down / step / up
Start by going down on mode 1, then up on mode 2, etc.

Take note of the direction arrows to the left of each diagram as well as the little arch above or below certain dots indicating a position shift using the same finger.

SUMMARY
Here are the 7th chords found on each mode.

Ionian	Dorian	Phrygian	Lydian	Mixolydian	Aeolian	Locrian
Maj7	min7	sus4♭9	Maj7♭5	Dom7 or 7sus4	min♭6	half-dim

Practice tip:
Once you can play these scales horizontally as one family, as shown in the following pages, then practice each horizontal model family (including arpeggios) starting from an open strings mode and then move horizontally to the next related mode in the correct order.

i.e.

E (open)	F	F#	G	G#	A	A#/B♭	B	C	C#	D	D#	E
Major		Dorian		Phrygian	Lydian		Mixo-lyd.		Aeolian		Locrian	Major
Dorian		Phrygian	Lydian		Mixo-lyd.		Aeolian		Locrian	Major		Dorian
Phrygian	Lydian		Mixo-lyd.		Aeolian		Locrian	Major		Dorian		Phrygian
Lydian		Mixo-lyd.		Aeolian		Locrian	Major		Dorian		Phrygian	Lydian
Mixolydian		Aeolian		Locrian	Major		Dorian		Phrygian	Lydian		Mixo-lyd.
Aeolian		Locrian	Major		Dorian		Phrygian	Lydian		Mixo-lyd.		Aeolian
Locrian	Major		Dorian		Phrygian	Lydian		Mixo-lyd.		Aeolian		Locrian

Now do the same excercise starting on the 1st position to cover all 12 keys.

The 7 modes generated by the Major Scale played
HORIZONTALLY – UP / step / DOWN

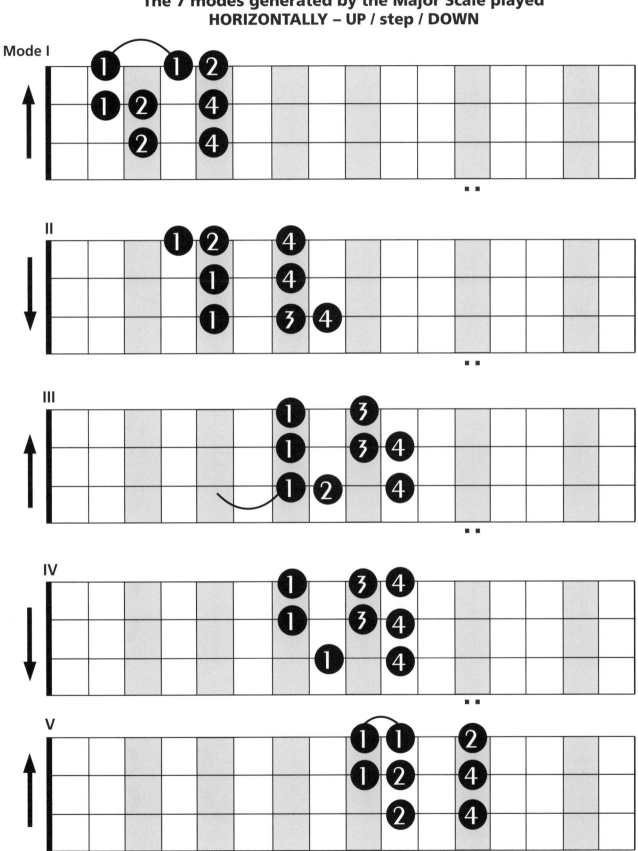

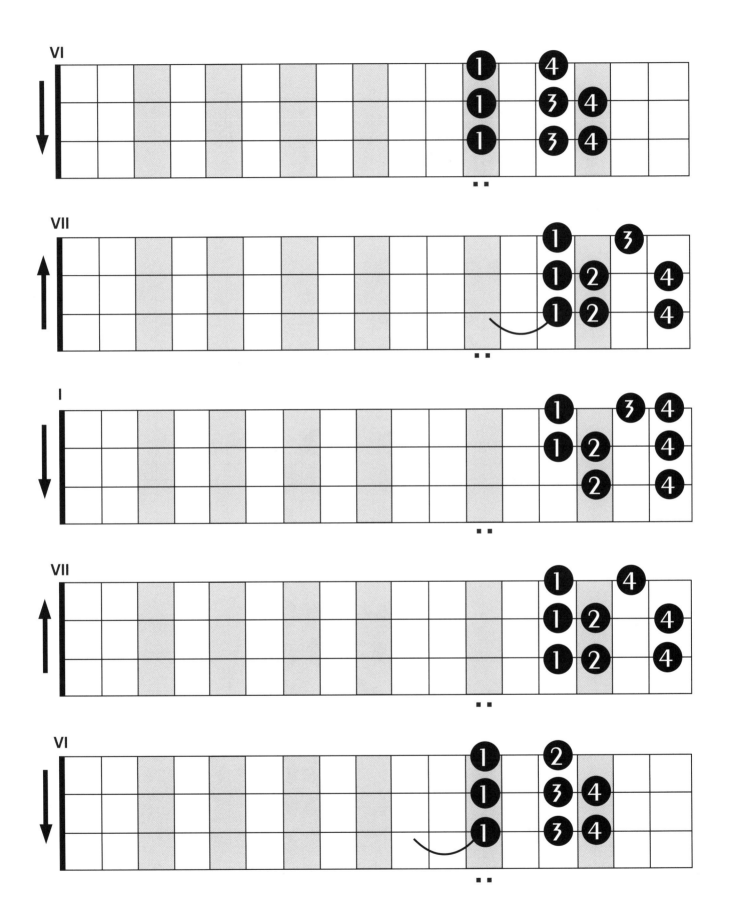

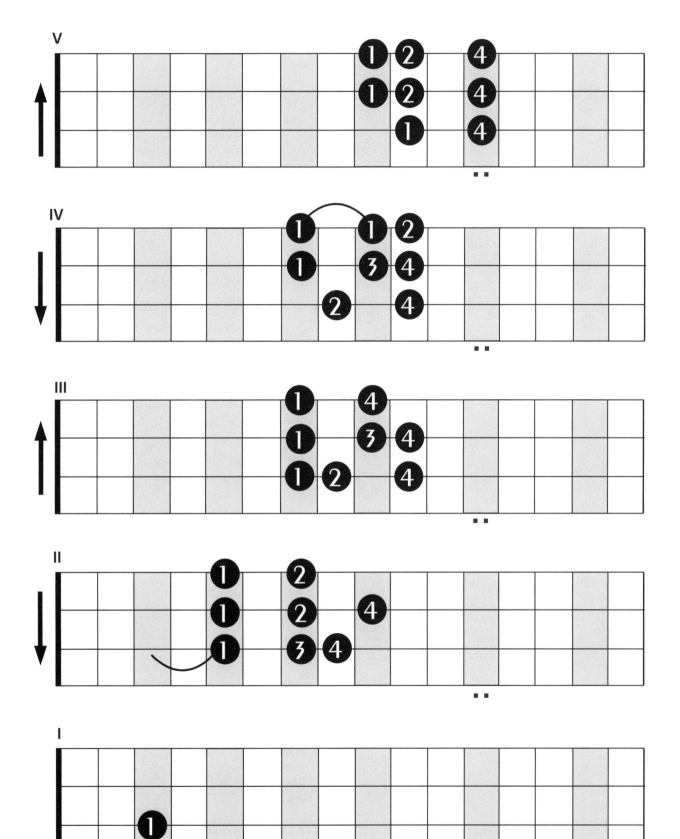

The 7 modes generated by the Major Scale played
HORIZONTALLY – DOWN / step / UP

Mode I

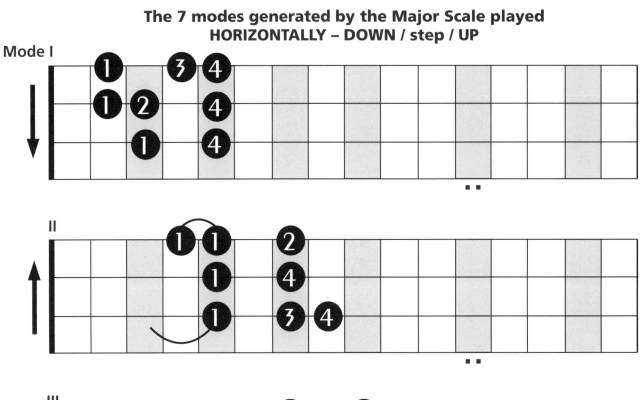

II

III

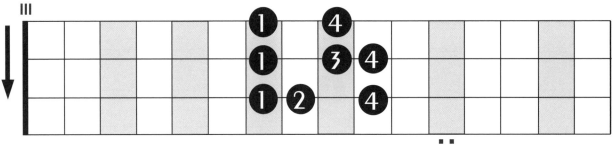

IV

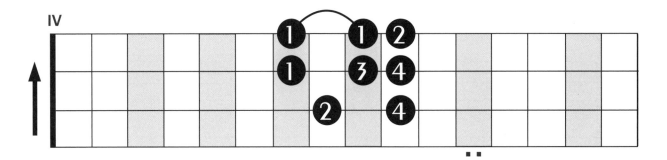

V

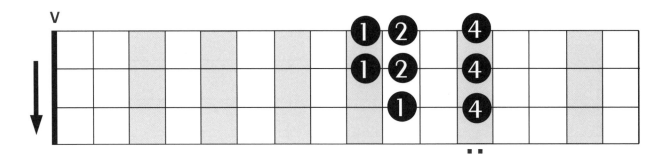

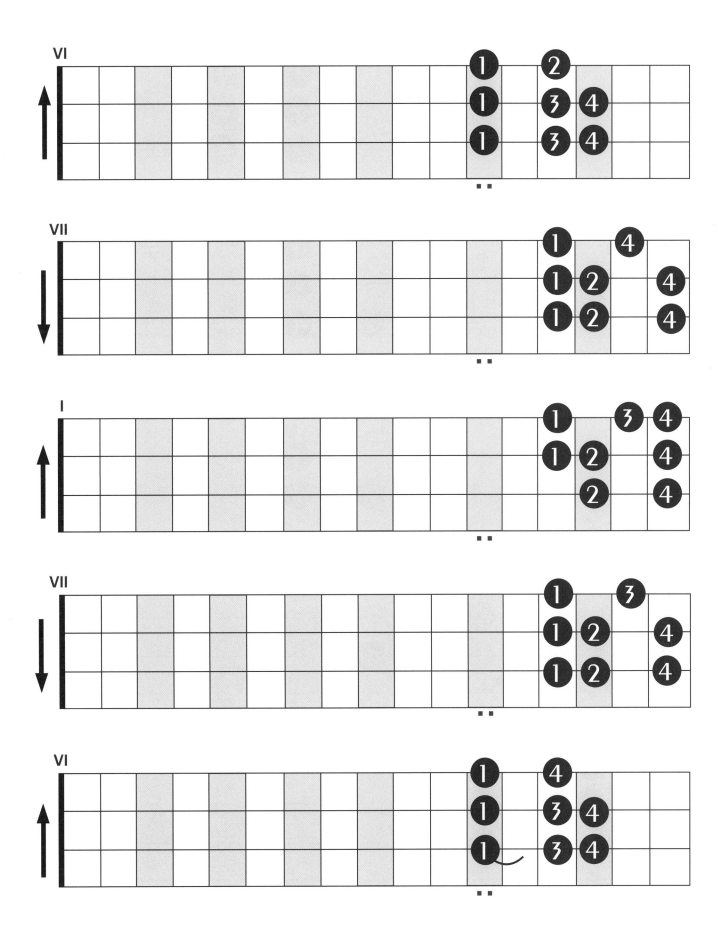

V

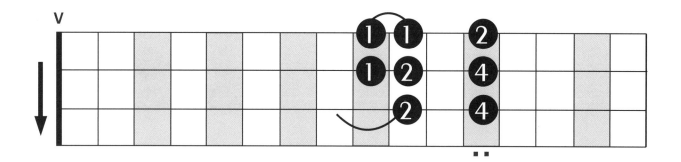

IV

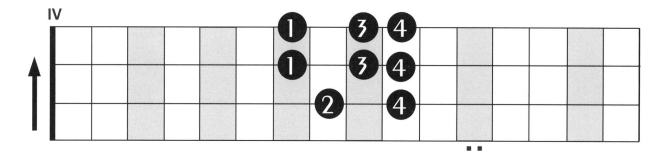

III

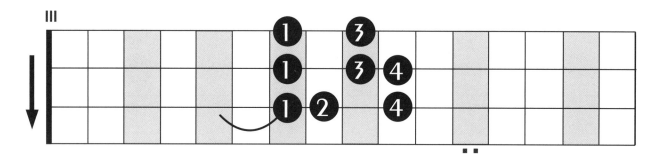

II

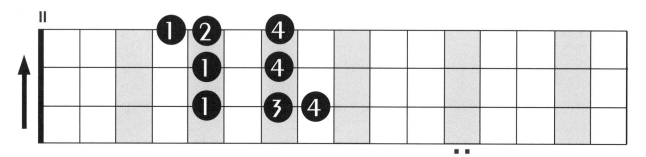

I

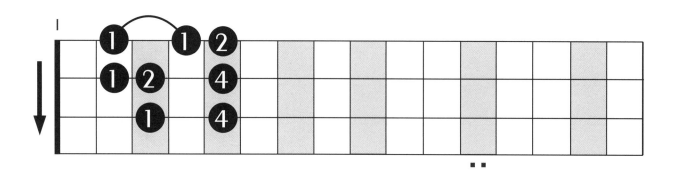

The SEVENTH ARPEGGIOS of the 7 modes generated by the Major Scale played HORIZONTALLY – UP / step / DOWN

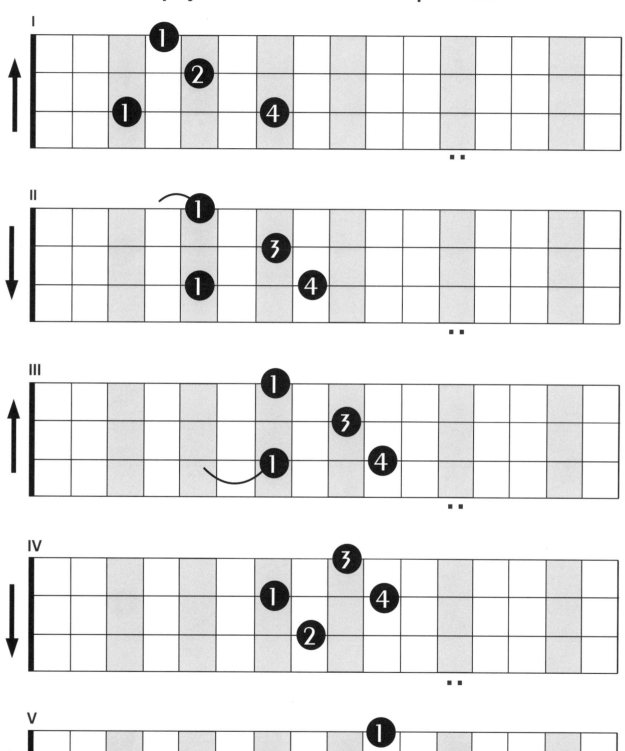

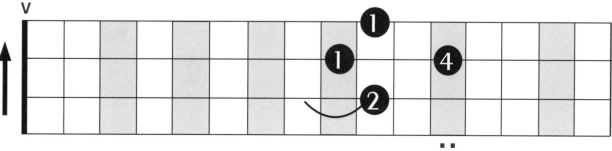

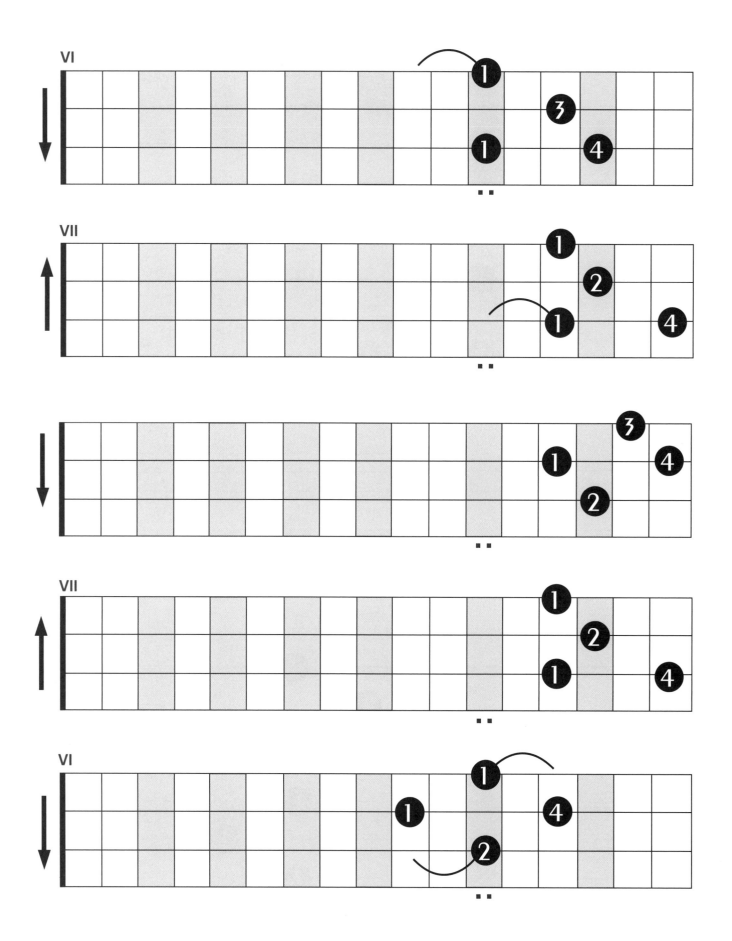

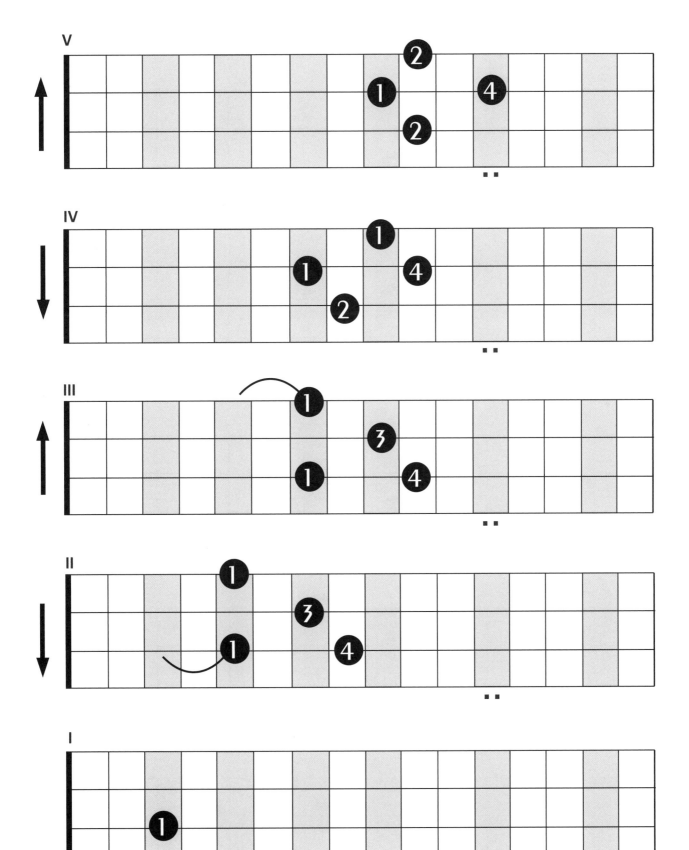

The SEVENTH ARPEGGIOS of the 7 modes generated by the Major Scale played HORIZONTALLY – DOWN / step / UP

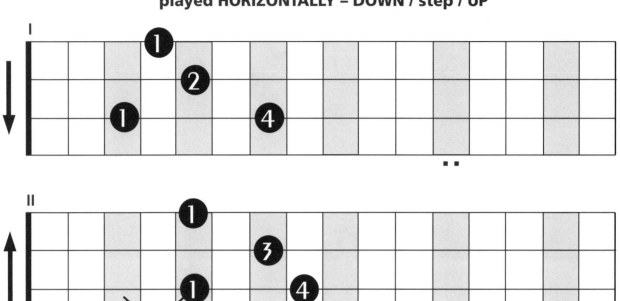

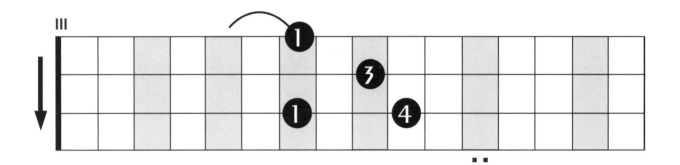

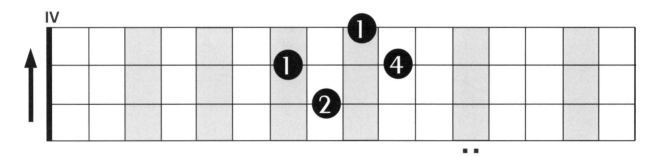

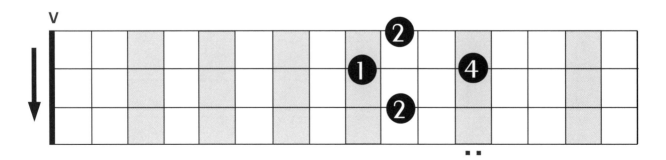

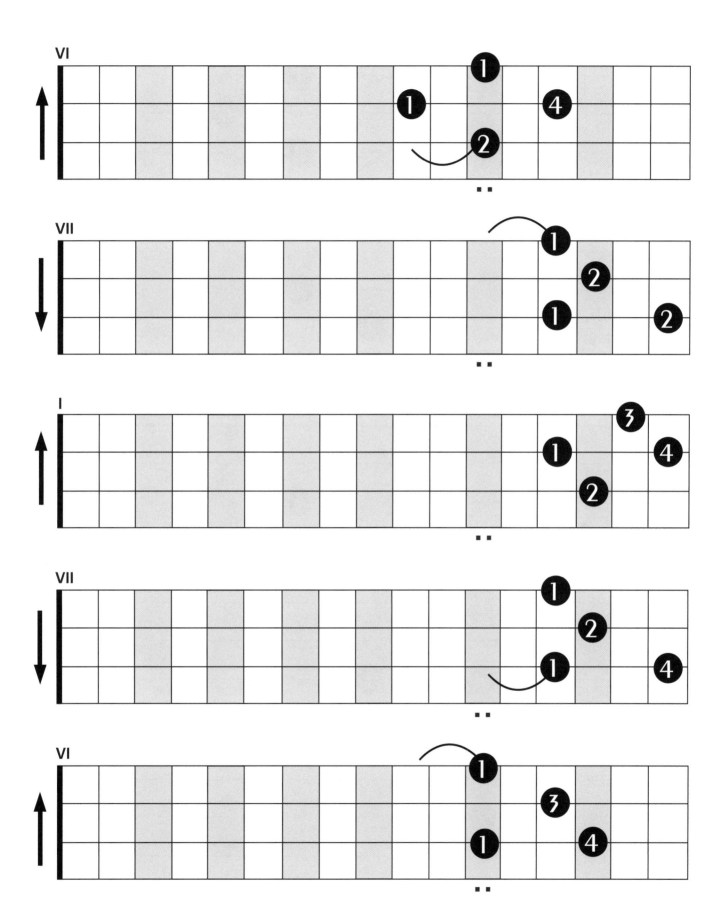

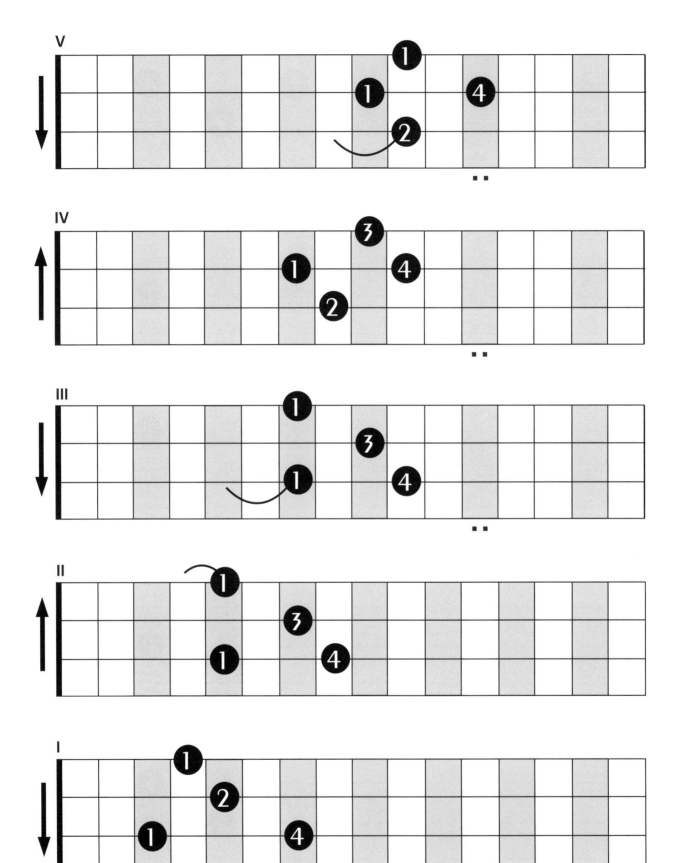

Practice Tip

Practicing the horizontal modes and their arpeggios in twelve different keys every day is going to leave you no time to practice anything else. But if you practiced for six days and took the seventh day off, this would mean that you could practice twelve keys over six days, two keys per day as illustrated in the diagram below, and still have time to practice other things.

Day	Key	
Monday	F	B♭
Tuesday	E♭	A♭
Wednesday	D♭	G♭
Thursday	B	E
Friday	A	D
Saturday	G	C

While we are on the subject of practicing, let us take a look at vertical scale practicing. Scales and arpeggios should be practiced from every angle. Here are the variations. (Step implies semitone.)

1.   **UP and DOWN**
2.   **DOWN and UP**
3.   **UP / step / DOWN / step / UP etc.**
4.   **DOWN / step / UP / step / DOWN etc.**
5.   **UPs only**
6.   **DOWNs only**

Practice the scales and arpeggios with the above variations moving up or down the neck in CHROMATIC STEPS or moving around the CYCLES*, excluding variation 3 & 4 on cycles. Once you can play the scales and arpeggios at a good tempo with a nice legato feel, you should then practise them in INTERVALLIC and SCALAR patterns (see page 234). This is a more musical way of practising them.

* See page 195

2.2
PENTATONIC and BLUES SCALES

MAJOR PENTATONIC SCALE

HARMONIC SPELLING: 1 – 2 – 3 – 5 – 6 – octave
CHORD FAMILY: Maj6/9, Maj7, Dom7
NOTE: If we were to play all the notes of this scale at the same time we would have a Maj6/9 chord.

C Major Pentatonic (neck position)

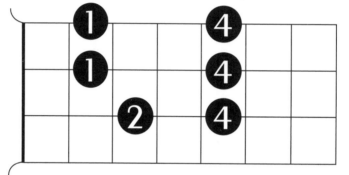

B♭ Major Pentatonic (1st position)

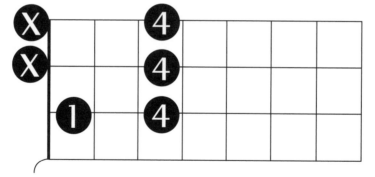

A Major Pentatonic (open position)

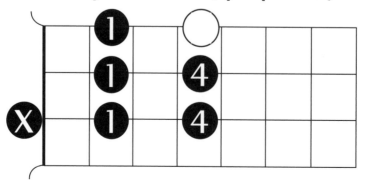

MINOR PENTATONIC

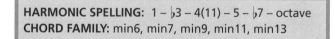

HARMONIC SPELLING: 1 – ♭3 – 4(11) – 5 – ♭7 – octave
CHORD FAMILY: min6, min7, min9, min11, min13

C Minor Pentatonic (neck position)

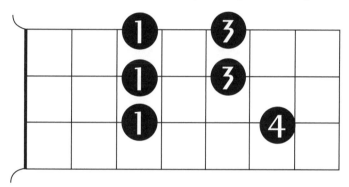

A Minor Pentatonic (open position)

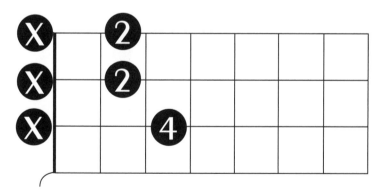

The 5 positions (modes) of the PENTATONIC SCALE

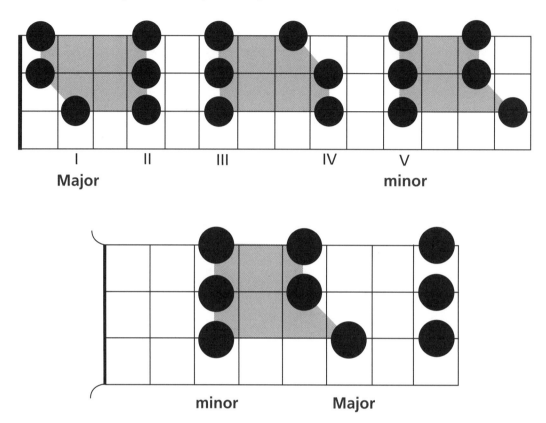

THE BLUES SCALE

HARMONIC SPELLING: 1 – ♭3 – 4 – #4 – 5 – ♭7 – octave
CHORD FAMILY: min7, Dom7 family chords

C Blues (neck position)

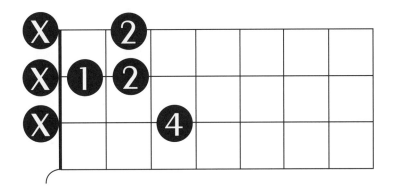

A Blues (open position)

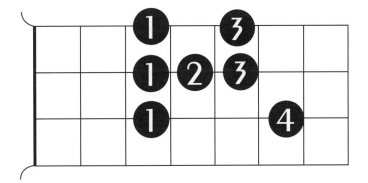

2.3
HARMONIC MINOR

HARMONIC MINOR SCALE

HARMONIC SPELLING: 1 – 2(9) – ♭3 – 4(11) – 5 – ♭6 – 7 – octave
ARPEGGIO: 1 – ♭3 – 5 – 7
CHORD FAMILY: min/Maj7

C Harmonic minor (neck position)

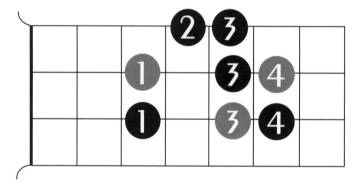

A Harmonic minor (open position)

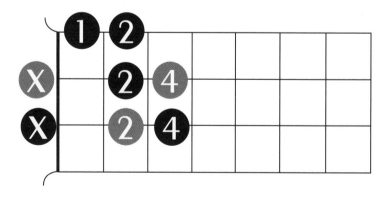

PHRYGIAN #3 SCALE

5th mode of the harmonic minor scale
Also known as the SPANISH SCALE

> **HARMONIC SPELLING:** 1 – ♭2(♭9) – 3 – 4(11) – 5 – ♭6 – ♭7 – octave
> **ARPEGGIO:** 1 – (♭9) – 3 – 5 – ♭7
> **CHORD FAMILY:** Dom7♭9, Dom7(♭9#5)
> **NOTE:** Can be played on the V chord of a minor II–V–I progression.

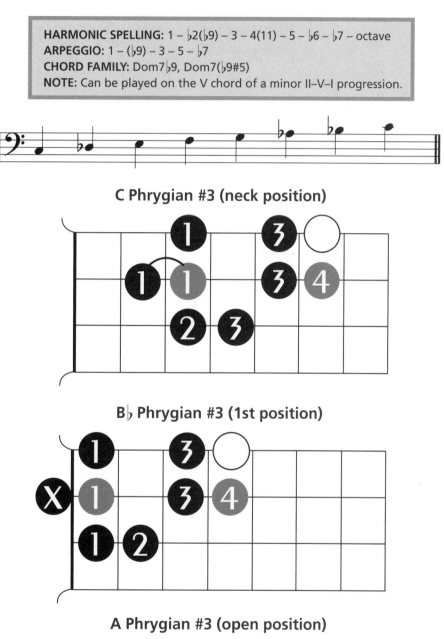

C Phrygian #3 (neck position)

B♭ Phrygian #3 (1st position)

A Phrygian #3 (open position)

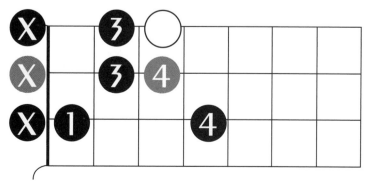

2.4
SYMMETRICAL SCALES

CHROMATIC SCALE
Symmetrical pattern: semitones

C Chromatic (neck position)

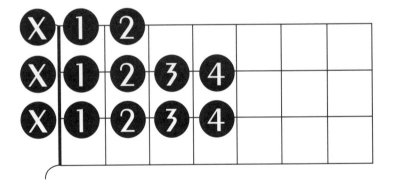

A Chromatic (open position)

WHOLE TONE SCALE
Symmetrical pattern: whole tones
This scale has six notes

HARMONIC SPELLING: 1 – 2(9) – 3 – #4(#11) – #5 – ♭7 – octave
ARPEGGIO: 1 – 3 – #5 – ♭7
CHORD FAMILY: Aug7, Dom7(#5,#11)
CHORD PROGRESSION: Can be used as a V chord in a major cadence.

C Whole tone (neck position)

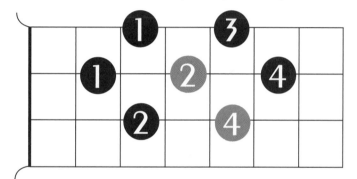

B♭ Whole tone (1st position)

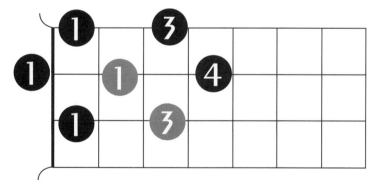

A Whole tone (open position)

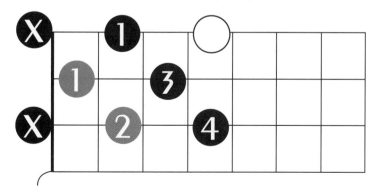

DIMINISHED SCALE

Symmetrical pattern: whole tone – semitone
This scale has eight notes.

HARMONIC SPELLING: 1 – 2(9) – ♭3 – 4(11) – ♭5 – ♭6(♭13) – ♭♭7 – 7 – octave
ARPEGGIO: 1 – ♭3 – ♭5 – ♭♭7
CHORD FAMILY: dim7

C Diminished (neck position)

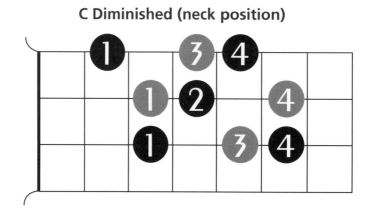

B♭ Diminished (1st position)

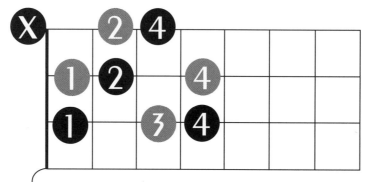

A Diminished (open position)

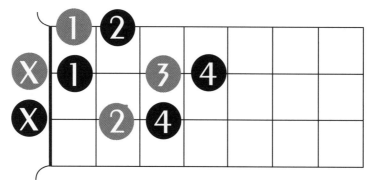

THE DIMINISHED BLUES SCALE
Also known as the
HALF-STEP / WHOLE-STEP DIMINISHED or The 8 NOTE DOMINANT SCALE
Symmetrical pattern: semitone – whole tone

HARMONIC SPELLING: 1 – (♭9) – (#9) – 3 – #4 (#11) – 5 – 6 – ♭7 – octave
CHORD FAMILY: Dom7 (♭5, ♭9, #9, #11)
NOTE: There is no #5.
SPELLING: Because this scale has 8 notes, an alphabet note (besides the root) has to be repeated in the spelling of the scale.
CHORD PROGRESSION: Can be used on the V chord of the II-V-I progression.

C Diminished Blues scale (neck position)

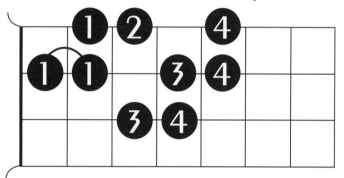

B♭ Diminished Blues scale (1st position)

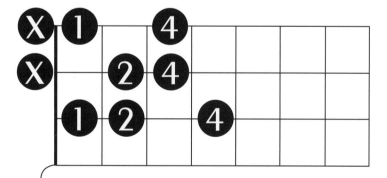

A Diminished Blues scale (open position)

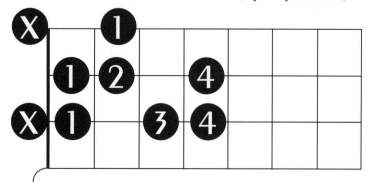

2.5.
MODES GENERATED BY THE ASCENDING MELODIC MINOR SCALE

MELODIC MINOR (ascending)
mode 1

HARMONIC SPELLING: 1 – 2(9) – ♭3 – 4(11) – 5 – 6 – 7 – octave
ARPEGGIO: 1 – ♭3 – 5 – 7
CHORD FAMILY: min/Maj7
SHORTCUT TIP: A shortcut to the Melodic minor is to play a Major scale and lower the 3rd to a minor 3rd.

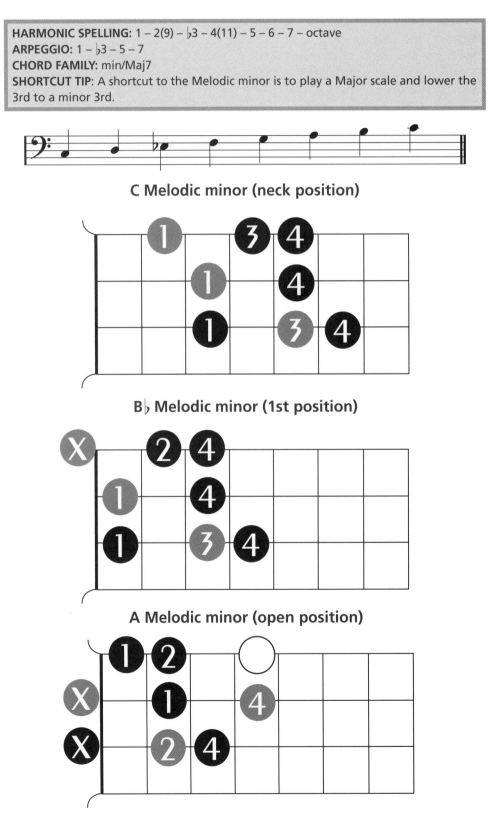

C Melodic minor (neck position)

B♭ Melodic minor (1st position)

A Melodic minor (open position)

DORIAN ♭9 SCALE
mode 2

> **HARMONIC SPELLING:** 1 – ♭2(♭9) – b3 – 4 – 5 – 6 – ♭7 – octave
> **ARPEGGIO:** 1 – ♭9 – 4 – 5 – ♭7
> **CHORD FAMILY:** sus♭9

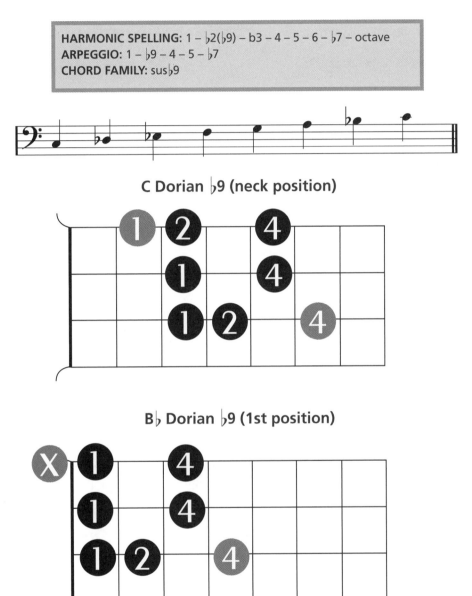

C Dorian ♭9 (neck position)

B♭ Dorian ♭9 (1st position)

A Dorian ♭9 (open position)

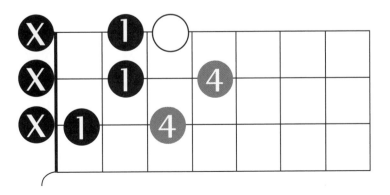

LYDIAN AUGMENTED SCALE
mode 3

HARMONIC SPELLING: 1 – 2(9) – 3 – #4(#11) – #5 – 6 – 7 – octave
ARPEGGIO: 1 – 3 – #5 – 7
CHORD FAMILY: Maj7#5
NOTE: Notice that the scale has a #11 which is not found in the chord.

C Lydian augmented (neck position)

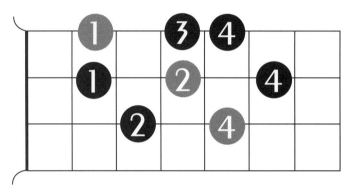

B♭ Lydian augmented (1st position)

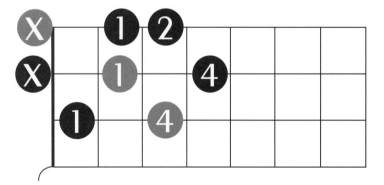

A Lydian augmented (open position)

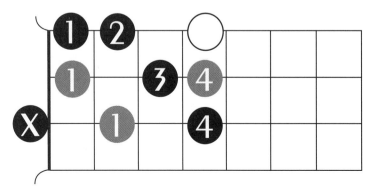

LYDIAN DOMINANT SCALE
mode 4

Also known as the LYDIAN ♭7 or MIXOLYDIAN #4 SCALE

> **HARMONIC SPELLING:** 1 –2(9) – 3 – #4(#11) – 5 – 6 – ♭7 – octave
> **ARPEGGIO:** 1 – 3 – ♭5 – ♭7
> **CHORD FAMILY:** Dom7#11, Dom13

C Lydian Dominant (neck position)

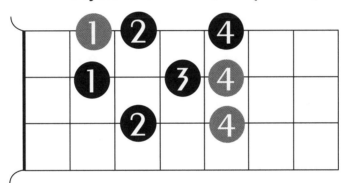

B♭ Lydian Dominant (1st position)

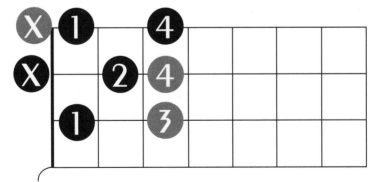

A Lydian Dominant (open position)

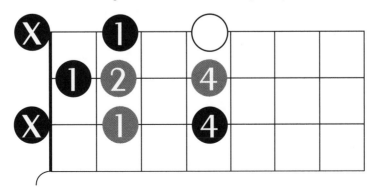

MIXOLYDIAN ♭13
mode 5

HARMONIC SPELLING: 1 –2(9) – 3 – 4 – 5 – ♭6(♭13) – ♭7 – octave
CHORD FAMILY: Dom7#5, Dom7♭13

C Mixolydian ♭13 (neck position)

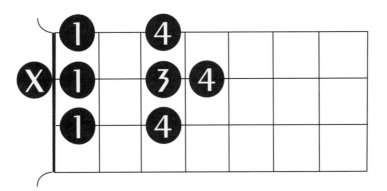

B♭ Mixolydian ♭13 (1st position)

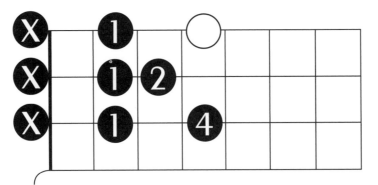

A Mixolydian ♭13 (open position)

LOCRIAN #2
mode 6

HARMONIC SPELLING: 1 – 2(9) – ♭3 – 4(11) – ♭5 – ♭6 – ♭7 – octave
ARPEGGIO: 1 – ♭3 – ♭5 – ♭7
CHORD FAMILY: min9♭5, (also written: Ø9)
NOTE: This is a half-diminished scale and chord with a natural 9.
CHORD PROGRESSION: The Locrian #2 scale can be used on the II chord of a minor II–V–I progression.

C Locrian #2 (neck position)

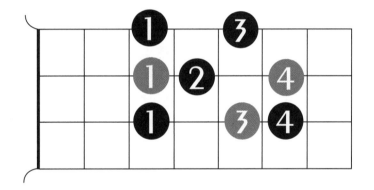

A Locrian #2 (open position)

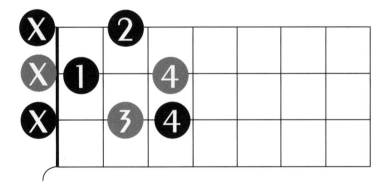

ALTERED SCALE
mode 7

Also known as THE SUPER LOCRIAN or the DIMINISHED WHOLE-TONE SCALE

SCALE: 1 – ♭2 – ♭3 – ♭4 – ♭5 – ♭6 – ♭7 – octave
HARMONIC SPELLING: 1 – (♭9) – (#9) – 3 – #4(#11) – #5 – ♭7 – octave
CHORD FAMILY: Dominant chords which have altered 5ths and 9ths, i.e. (♭5/♭9, ♭5/#9, #5/♭9, #5/#9). Also known as an altered dominant chord, written C7alt.
CHORD PROGRESSION: This scale can be used on the V chord of a minor II–V–I progression.

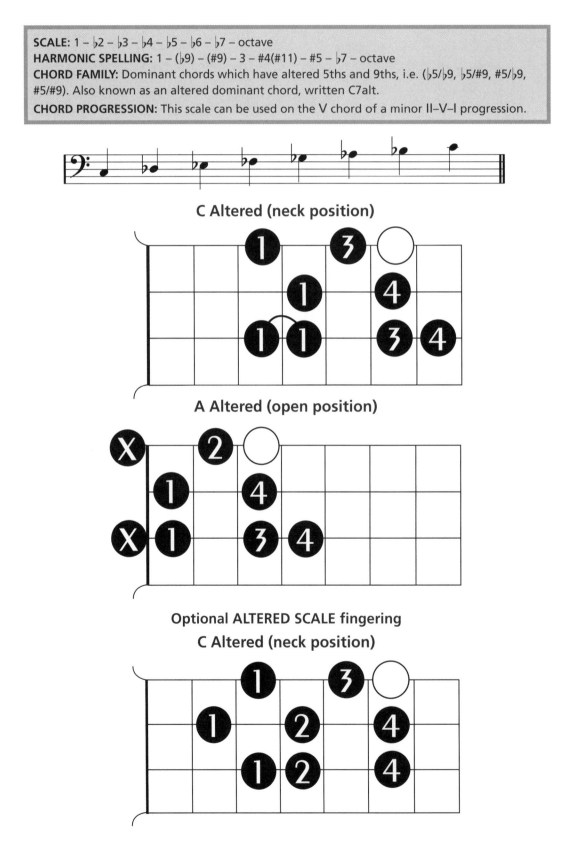

C Altered (neck position)

A Altered (open position)

Optional ALTERED SCALE fingering
C Altered (neck position)

2.6
BEBOP SCALES
Note: There are more than these three.

BEBOP MAJOR SCALE

> **NOTE:** The chromatic passing note in the Bebop Major Scale is between the 5th and the 6th, indicated by the grey dot.

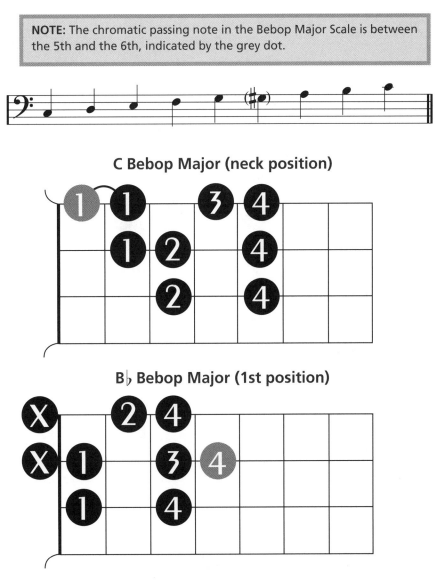

C Bebop Major (neck position)

B♭ Bebop Major (1st position)

A Bebop Major (open position)

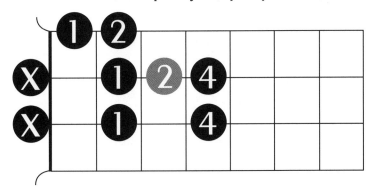

BEBOP DORIAN SCALE

NOTE: The chromatic passing note in the Bebop Dorian Scale is between the 3rd and the 4th, indicated by the grey dot.

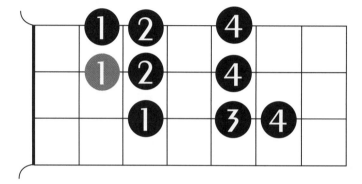

C Bebop Dorian (neck position)

Bb Bebop Dorian (1st position)

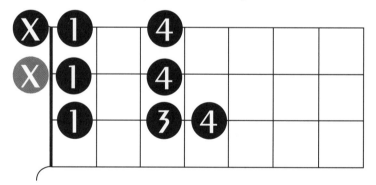

A Bebop Dorian (open position)

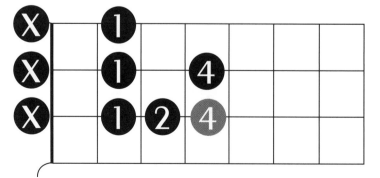

BEBOP MIXOLYDIAN SCALE

NOTE: The chromatic passing note in the Bebop Mixolydian Scale is between the 7th and the root, indicated by the grey dot.

C Bebop Mixolydian (neck position)

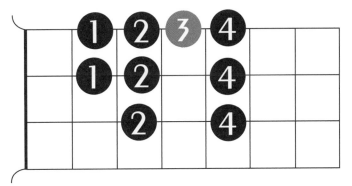

B♭ Bebop Mixolydian (1st position)

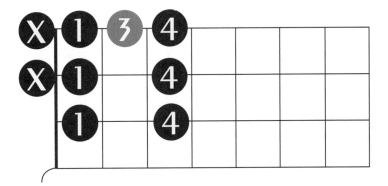

A Bebop Mixolydian (open position)

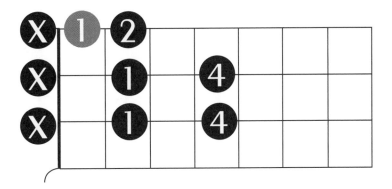

CHAPTER 3

VERTICAL SCALES on 4 STRINGS
(up to the 11th)

3.1
The 7 modes generated by the MAJOR SCALE

IONIAN (major) SCALE
mode 1

HARMONIC SPELLING: 1 – 2(9) – 3 – 4 – 5 – 6 – 7 – octave
ARPEGGIO: 1 – 3 – 5 – 7 – 9 – 11
CHORD FAMILY: Major chords, Maj7, Maj9, Maj6/9
PASSING TONE: 4th

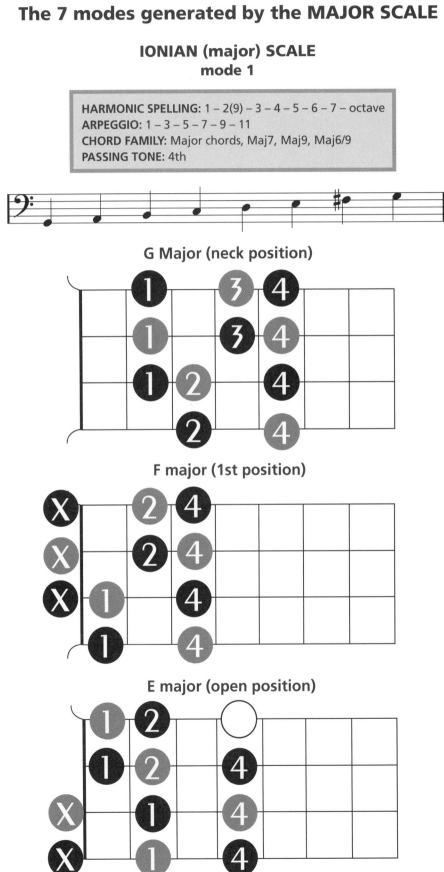

G Major (neck position)

F major (1st position)

E major (open position)

DORIAN SCALE
mode 2

HARMONIC SPELLING: 1 – 2(9) – ♭3 – 4(11) – 5 – 6(13) – ♭7 – octave
ARPEGGIO: 1 – ♭3 – 5 – ♭7 – 9 – 11
CHORD FAMILY: min6, min7, min9, min11, min13
CHORD PROGRESSION: The Dorian scale is used on minor I chords & the II chord of a
II–V–I progression.
SHORTCUT TIP: If we play any Aeolian scale and raise the 6th, we have the Dorian.

G Dorian (neck position)

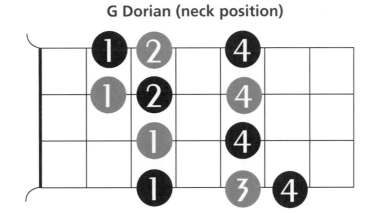

F Dorian (1st position)

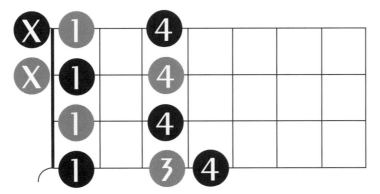

E Dorian (open position)

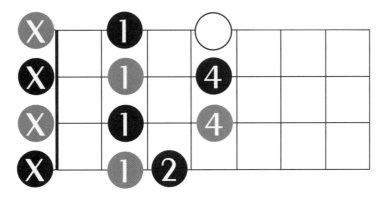

Optional DORIAN SCALE fingering

> **NOTE:** This fingering is useful when shifting between the modes, as well as when playing certain scalar and intervallic patterns.

G Dorian (neck position)

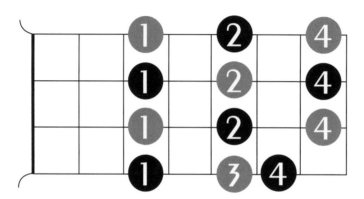

PHRYGIAN SCALE
mode 3

HARMONIC SPELLING: 1 – ♭2(♭9) – ♭3 – 4(11) – 5 – ♭6(♭13) – ♭7 – octave
ARPEGGIO: 1 – ♭3 – 5 – ♭7 – ♭9 – 11
CHORD FAMILY: sus4♭9
NOTE: Notes most often played on a sus ♭9 chord are root, ♭9, 4, 5, ♭7.
SHORTCUT TIP: Play an Aeolian scale and lower the 2nd note to get a Phrygian scale.

G Phrygian (neck position)

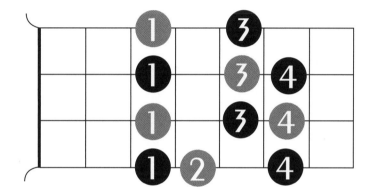

E Phrygian (open position)

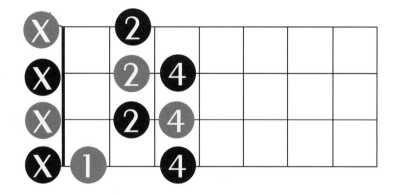

LYDIAN SCALE
mode 4

> **HARMONIC SPELLING:** 1 – 2(9) – 3 – #4(#11) – 5 – 6(13) – 7 – octave
> **ARPEGGIO:** 1 – 3 – 5 – 7 – 9 – #11
> **CHORD FAMILY:** Maj, Maj7, Maj7♭5, Maj7#11, Maj13#11

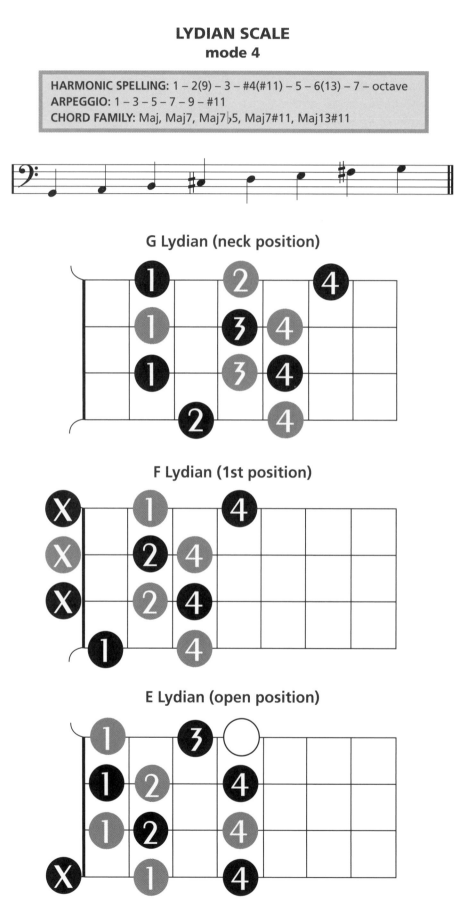

G Lydian (neck position)

F Lydian (1st position)

E Lydian (open position)

MIXOLYDIAN SCALE
mode 5

HARMONIC SPELLING: 1 – 2(9) – 3 – 4(11) – 5 – 6(13) – ♭7 – octave
ARPEGGIO: 1 – 3 – 5 – ♭7 – 9 – 11
CHORD FAMILY: Dom7, Dom9, Dom13, 7sus4
PASSING TONE (avoid note) is the 4th (excepting on a sus4 chord)
CHORD PROGRESSION: Can use the Mixolydian scale on dominant 7 chords, for example on the V7 chord of the II–V–I progression as well as on the blues.

G Mixolydian (neck position)

F Mixolydian (1st position)

E Mixolydian (open position)

AEOLIAN (natural minor) SCALE
mode 6
The relative minor of the Major Scale with the same key signature.

HARMONIC SPELLING: 1 – 2(9) – ♭3 – 4(11) – 5 – ♭6 – ♭7 – octave
ARPEGGIO: 1 – ♭3 – 5 – ♭7 – 9 – 11
CHORD FAMILY: min7, min9, min♭6

G Aeolian (neck position)

F Aeolian (1st position)

E Aeolian (open position)

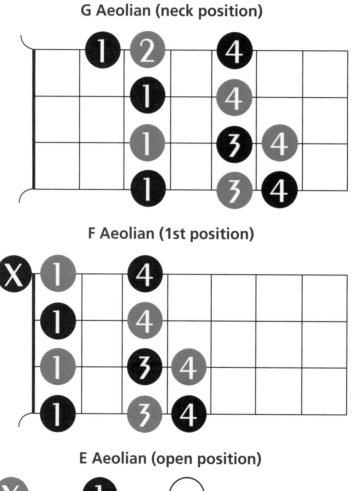

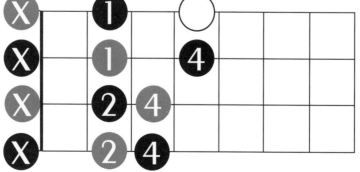

LOCRIAN SCALE
mode 7

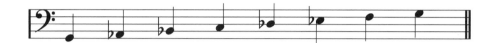

HARMONIC SPELLING: 1 – ♭2(♭9) – ♭3 – 4(11) – ♭5 – ♭6 – ♭7 – octave
ARPEGGIO: 1 – ♭3 – ♭5 – ♭7 – ♭9 – 11
CHORD FAMILY: min7♭5 or Ø (called a 'half-diminished')
PASSING TONE (avoid note) is the ♭9

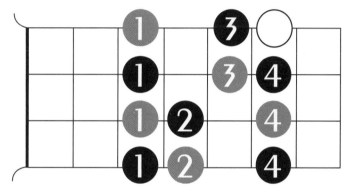

G Locrian (neck position)

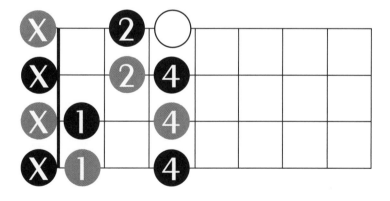

E Locrian (open position)

HORIZONTAL SHIFTING BETWEEN THE VERTICAL MODES & 7TH ARPEGGIOS OF THE MAJOR SCALE

There are two exercises here.

1. Up / step / down
First, go up on mode 1 then come down on mode 2, then up on mode 3, etc.

2. Down / step / up
Start by going down on mode 1, then up on mode 2, etc.

Take note of the direction arrows to the left of each diagram and the little arch above or below certain dots indicating a position shift using the same finger.

ARPEGGIOS
The 9th, and 11th arpeggios are easy to see on the vertical scales done so far, but they also have to be practiced horizontally and the fingering is a little different to the vertical fingering.

SUMMARY
Here are the 7th chords found on each mode.

Ionian	Dorian	Phrygian	Lydian	Mixolydian	Aeolian	Locrian
Maj7	min7	sus4 ♭9	Maj7♭5	Dom7 or 7sus4	min♭6	half-dim

Practice tip:
Once you can play these scales horizontally as one family as shown in the following pages, then practice each horizontal model family (including arpeggios) starting from an open strings mode and then move horizontally to the next related mode in the correct order.

i.e.

E (open)	F	F#	G	G#	A	A#/B♭	B	C	C#	D	D#	E
Major		Dorian		Phrygian	Lydian		Mixo-lyd.		Aeolian		Locrian	**Major**
Dorian		Phrygian	Lydian		Mixo-lyd.		Aeolian		Locrian	**Major**		Dorian
Phrygian	Lydian		Mixo-lyd.		Aeolian		Locrian	**Major**		Dorian		Phrygian
Lydian		Mixo-lyd.		Aeolian		Locrian	**Major**		Dorian		Phrygian	Lydian
Mixolydian		Aeolian		Locrian	**Major**		Dorian		Phrygian	Lydian		Mixo-lyd.
Aeolian		Locrian	**Major**		Dorian		Phrygian	Lydian		Mixo-lyd.		Aeolian
Locrian	**Major**		Dorian		Phrygian	Lydian		Mixo-lyd.		Aeolian		Locrian

Now do the same excercise starting on the 1st position to cover all 12 keys.

Next practice tip:
Follow the above routine, which starts on an open string mode, and play from the 11th of each vertical scale going down to the root. One pitch direction only, in other words, down – down – down, etc. This will really help you to internalise the horizontal modal family scales.

**The 7 modes generated by the Major scale played HORIZONTALLY –
UP / step / DOWN**

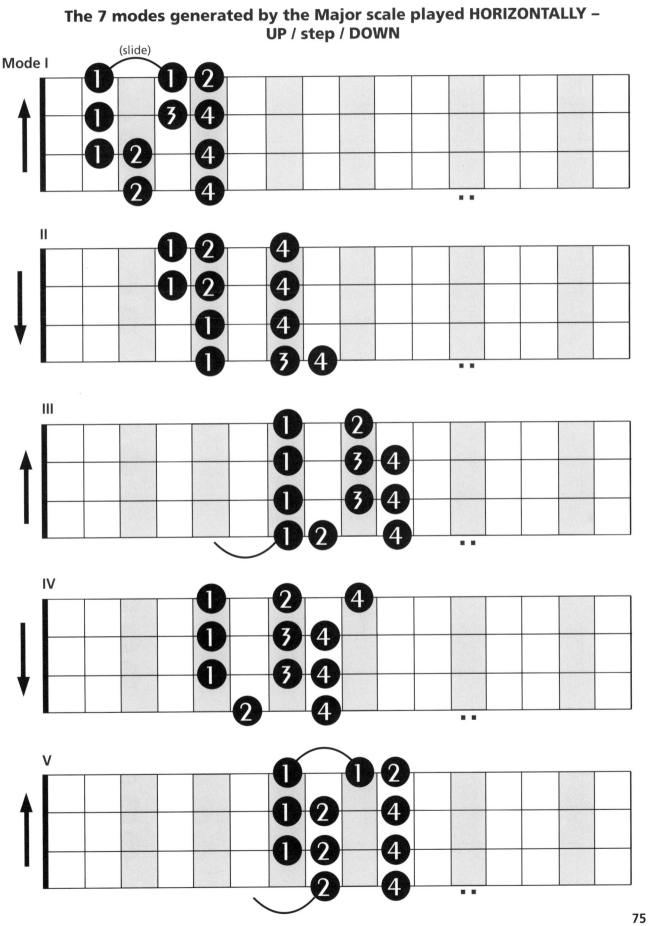

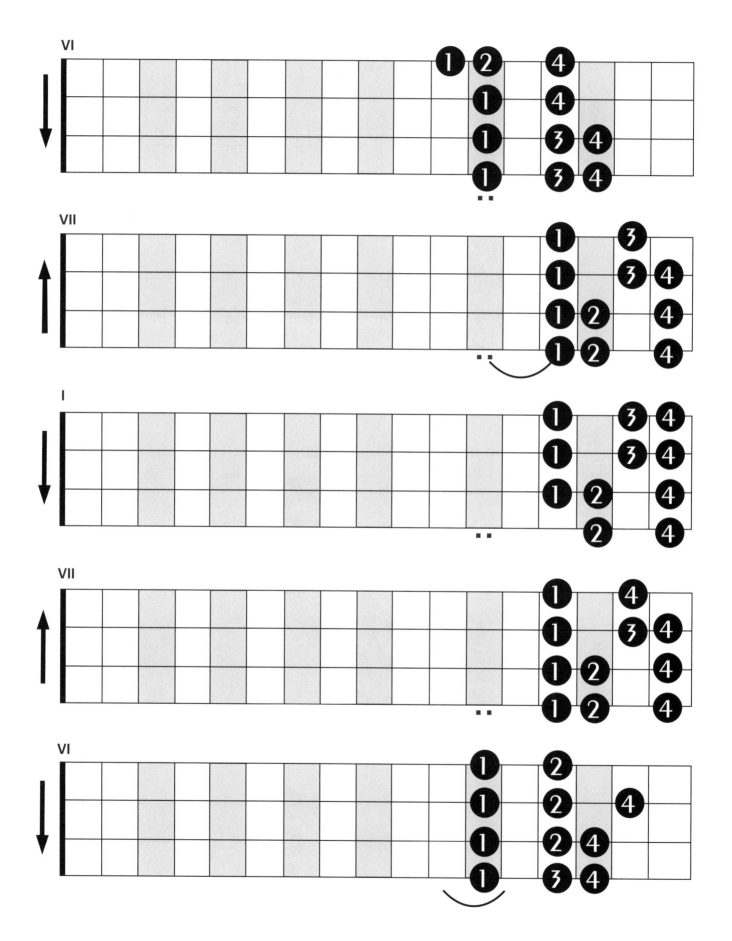

V

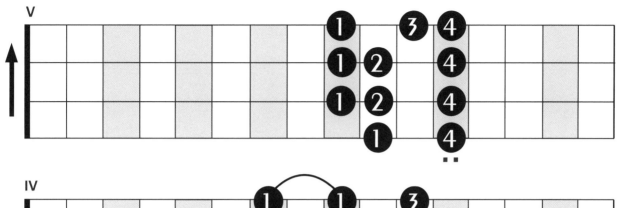

IV

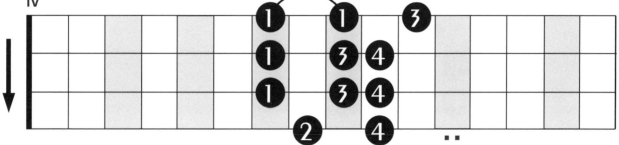

III

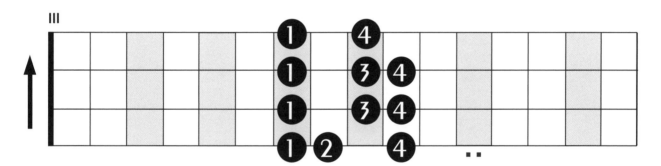

II

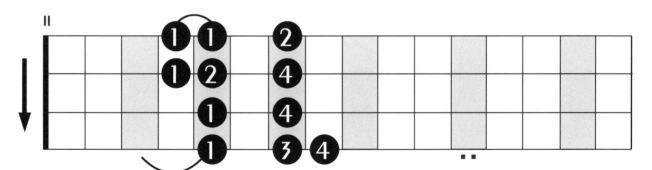

I

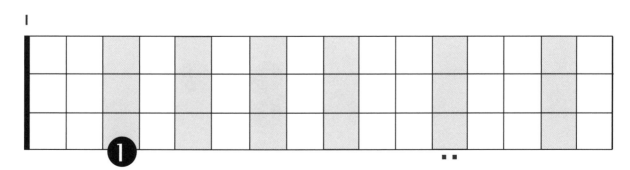

The 7 modes generated by the Major scale played HORIZONTALLY – DOWN / step / UP

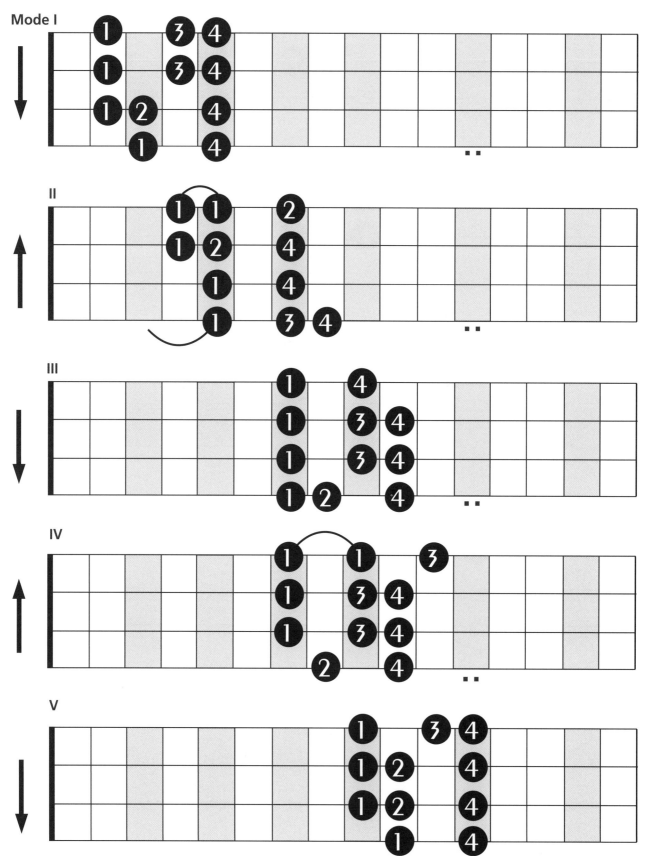

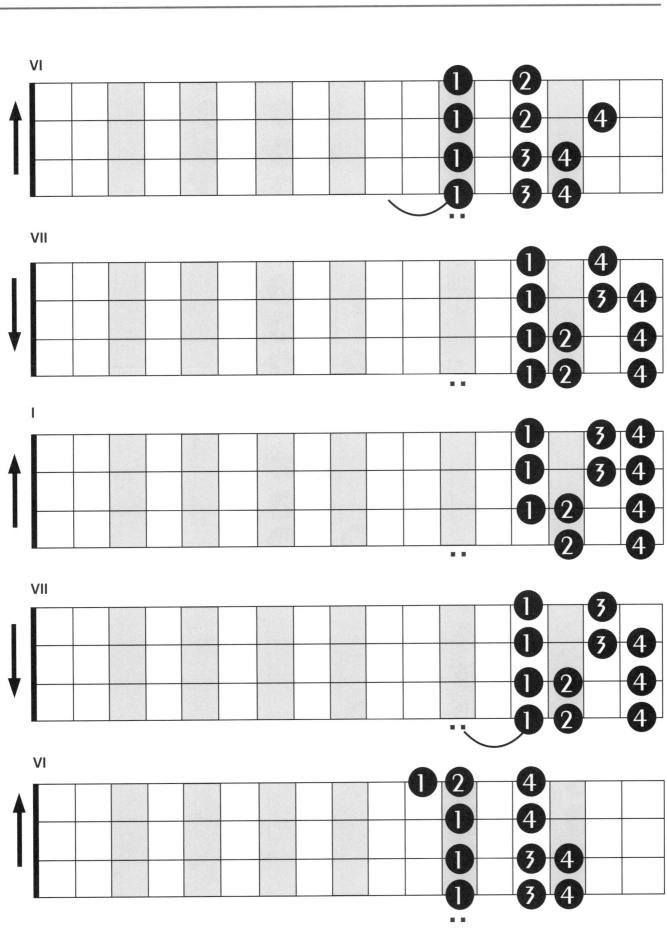

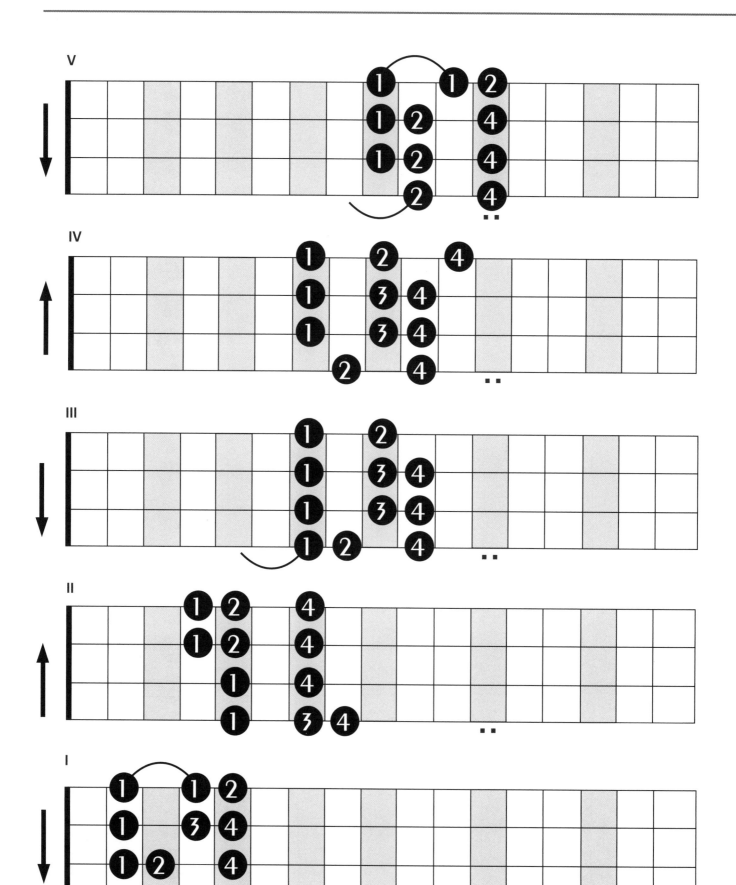

The 9th ARPEGGIOS of the Major scale modes played
HORIZONTALLY – UP / step / DOWN

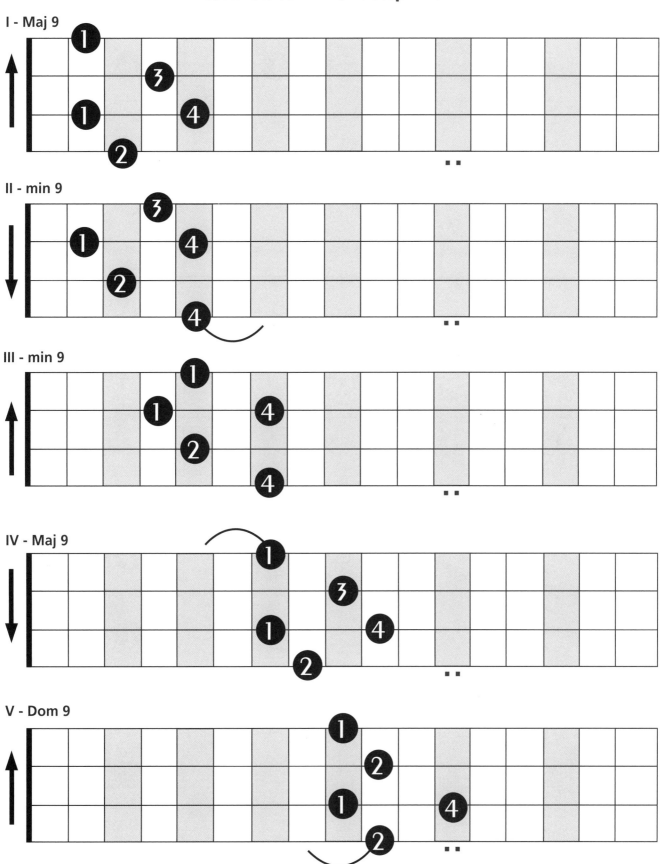

I - Maj 9

II - min 9

III - min 9

IV - Maj 9

V - Dom 9

VI - min 9

VII - half-dim 9

I - Maj 9

VII - half-dim 9

VI - min 9

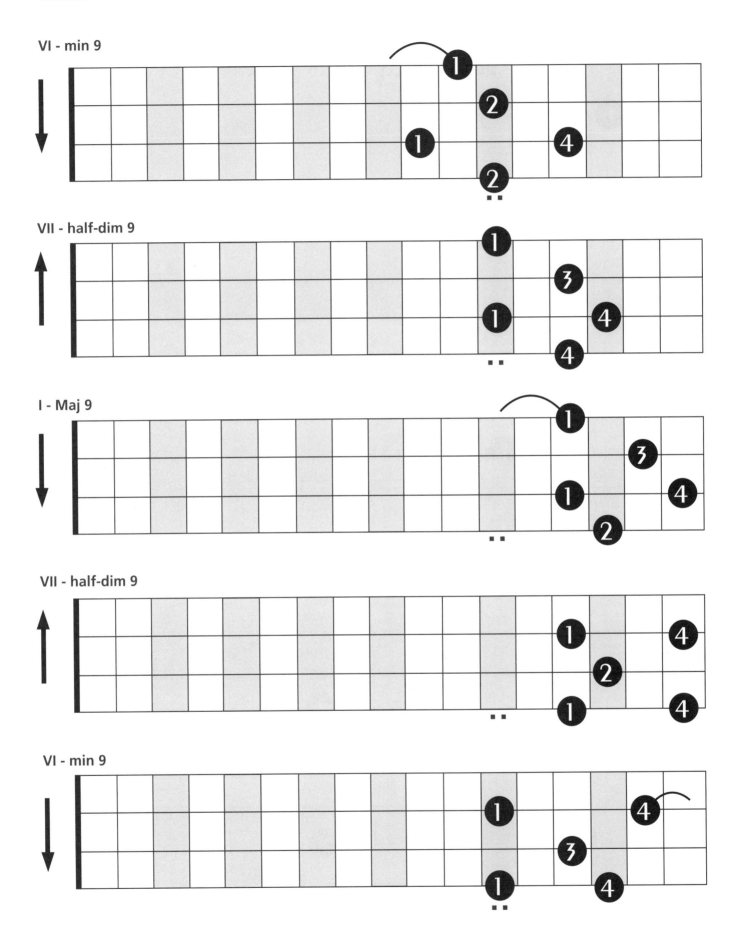

V - Dom 9

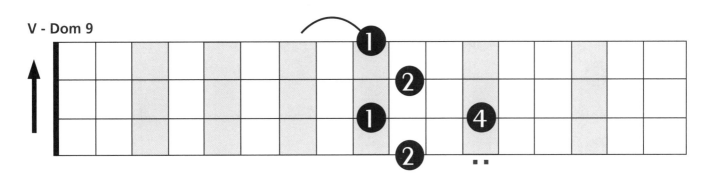

IV - Maj 9

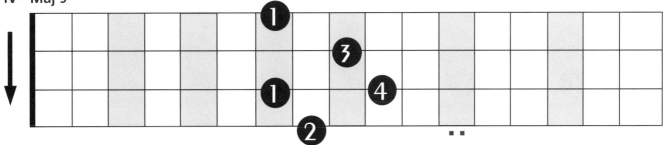

III - min 9

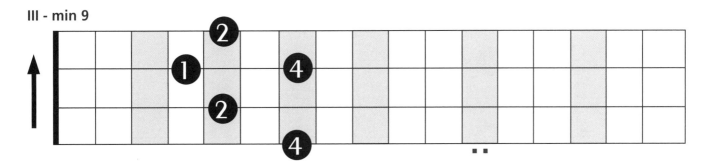

II - min 9

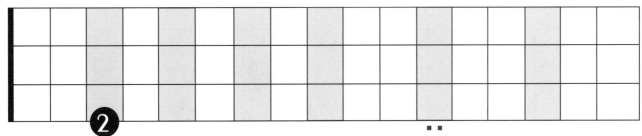

I - Maj 9

The 9th ARPEGGIOS of the Major scale modes played
HORIZONTALLY – DOWN / step / UP

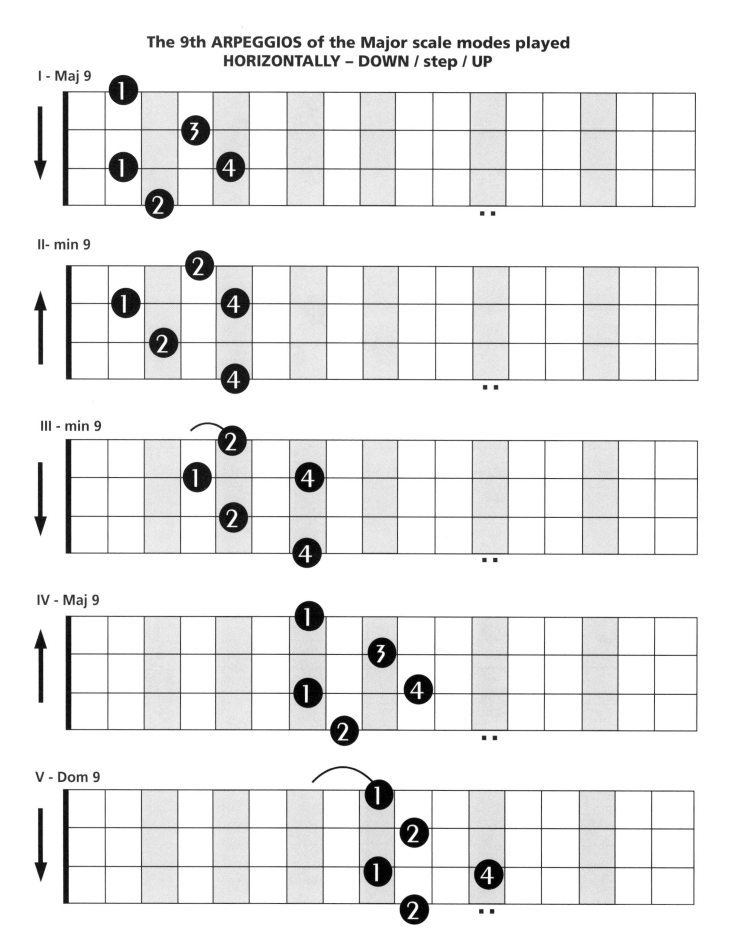

I - Maj 9

II- min 9

III - min 9

IV - Maj 9

V - Dom 9

VI - min 9

VII - half-dim 9

I - Maj 9

VII - half-dim 9

VI - min 9

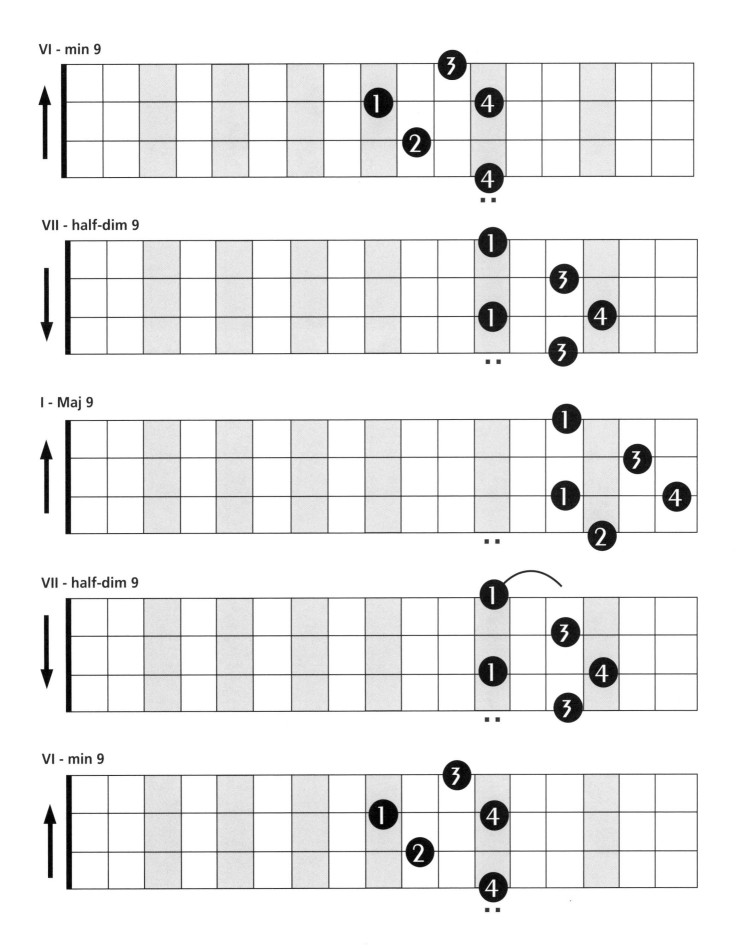

V - Dom 9

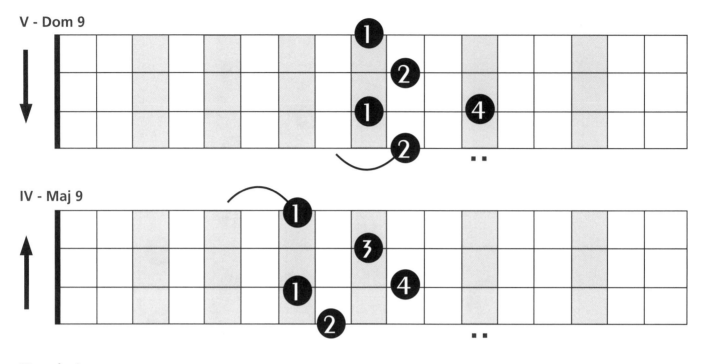

IV - Maj 9

III - min 9

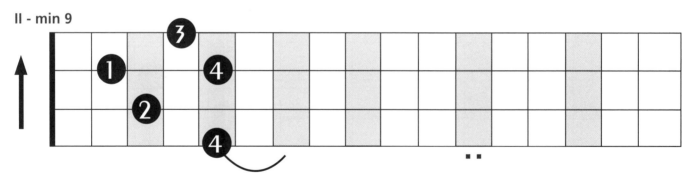

II - min 9

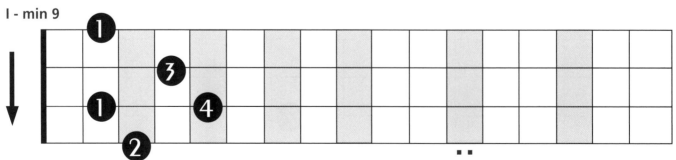

I - min 9

The 11th ARPEGGIOS of the Major scale modes played
HORIZONTAL – UP / step / DOWN

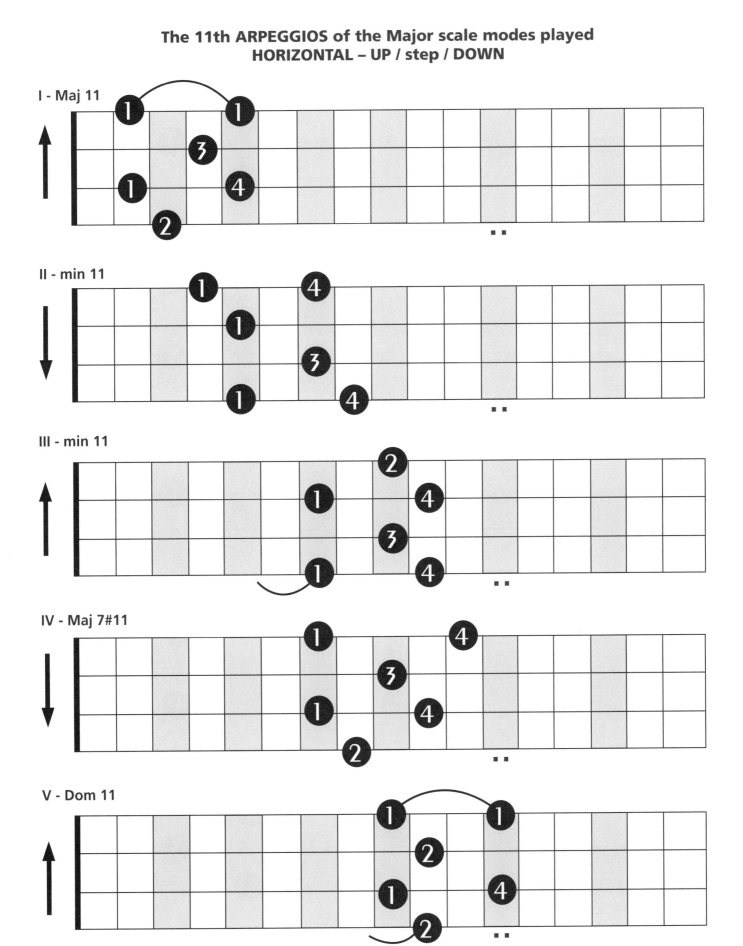

I - Maj 11

II - min 11

III - min 11

IV - Maj 7#11

V - Dom 11

VI - min 11

VII - half-dim 11

I - Maj 11

VII - half-dim 11

VI - min 11

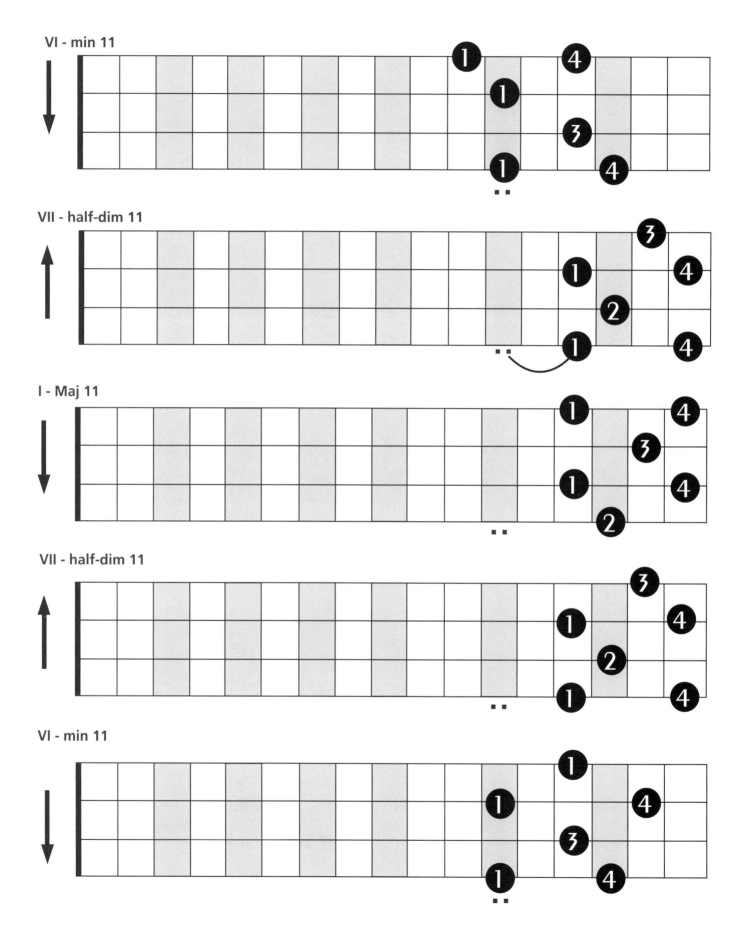

V - Dom 11

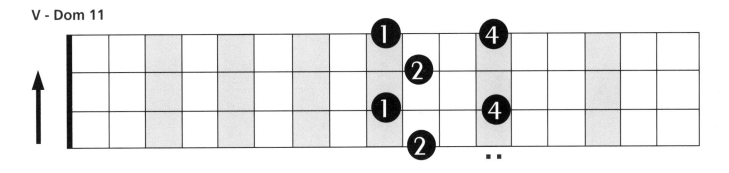

IV - Maj 7#11

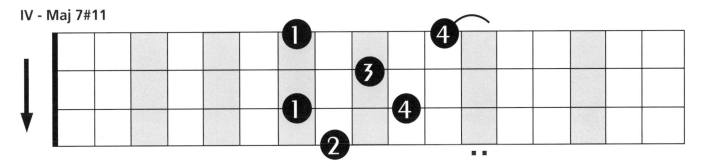

III - min 11

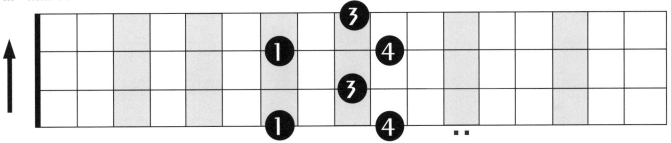

II - min 11

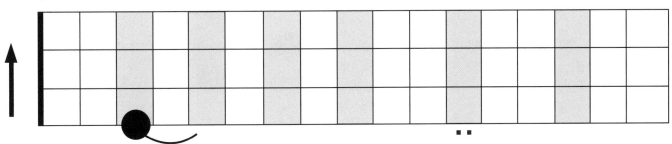

I - Maj 11

The 11th ARPEGGIOS of the modes generated by the Major scale, played HORIZONTALLY – DOWN / step / UP

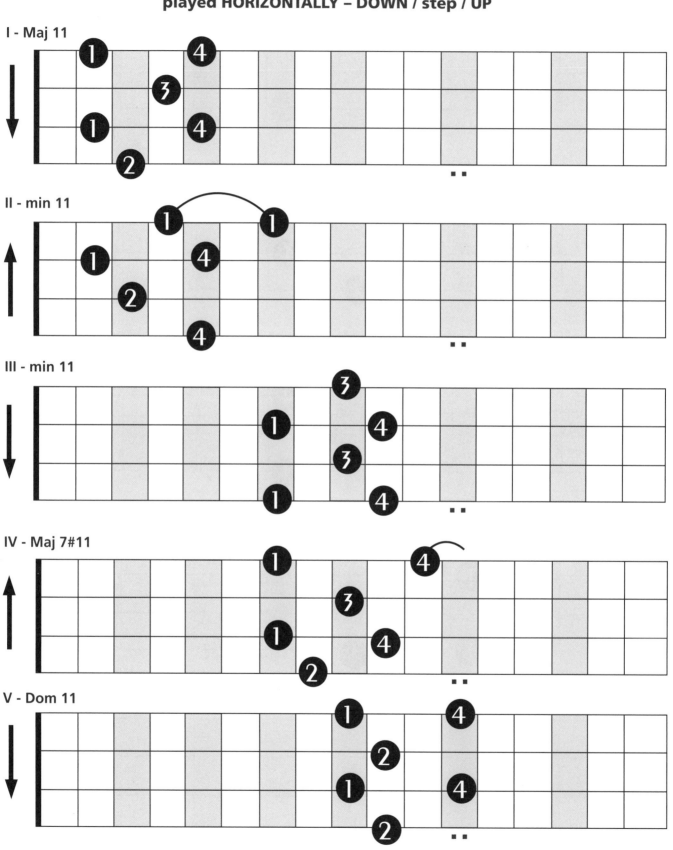

I - Maj 11

II - min 11

III - min 11

IV - Maj 7#11

V - Dom 11

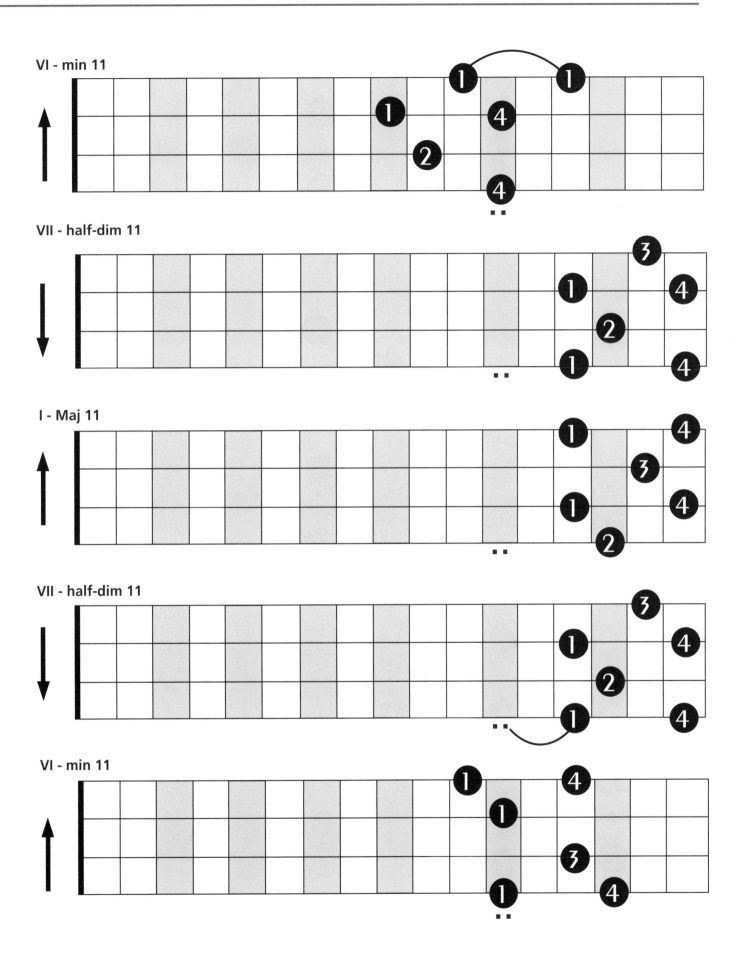

V - Dom 11

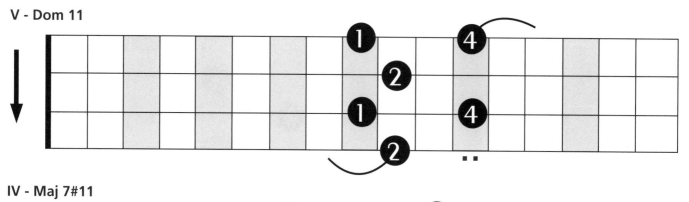

IV - Maj 7#11

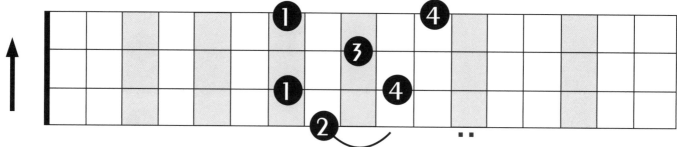

III - min 11

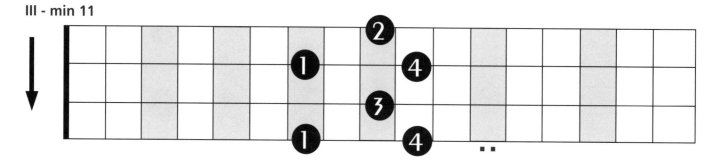

II - min 11

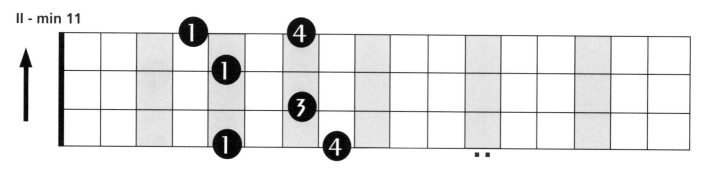

I - Maj 11

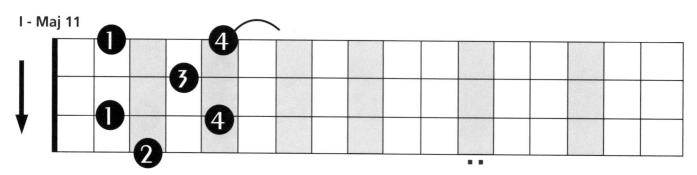

3.2
PENTATONIC and BLUES SCALES

MAJOR PENTATONIC SCALE

HARMONIC SPELLING: 1 – 2 – 3 – 5 – 6 – octave
CHORD FAMILY: Maj6/9, Maj7, Dom7
NOTE: If we were to play all the notes of this scale at the same time we would have a Maj6/9 chord.

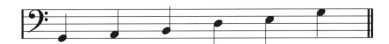

G Major Pentatonic (neck position)

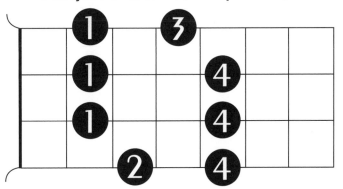

F Major Pentatonic (1st position)

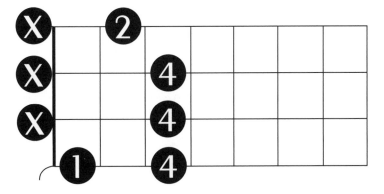

E Major Pentatonic (open position)

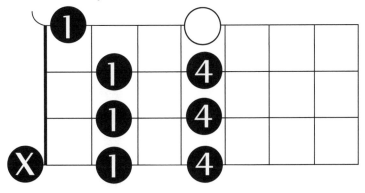

MINOR PENTATONIC

HARMONIC SPELLING: 1 – ♭3 – 4(11) – 5 – ♭7 – octave
CHORD FAMILY: min6, min7, min9, min11, min13

G Minor Pentatonic (neck position)

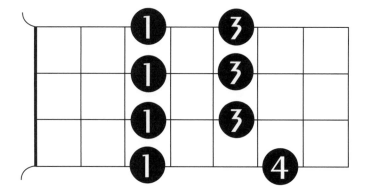

E Minor Pentatonic (open position)

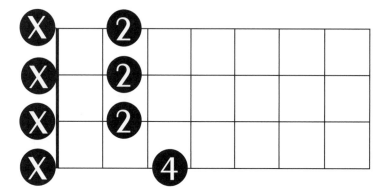

The 5 positions (modes) of the PENTATONIC SCALE

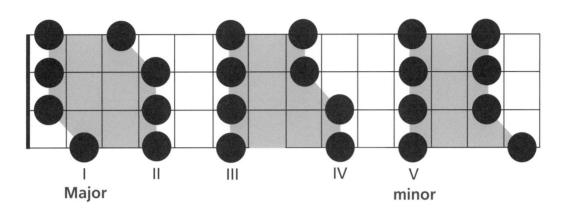

I   II   III   IV   V

Major   minor

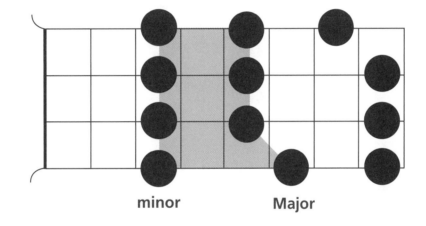

minor   Major

THE BLUES SCALE

HARMONIC SPELLING: 1 – ♭3 – 4 – #4 – 5 – ♭7 – octave
CHORD FAMILY: min7, Dom7 family chords

G Blues (neck position)

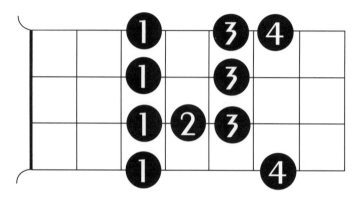

E Blues (open position)

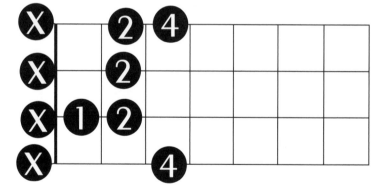

3.3
HARMONIC MINOR SCALE

HARMONIC MINOR

HARMONIC SPELLING: 1 – 2(9) – ♭3 – 4(11) – 5 – ♭6 – 7 – octave
ARPEGGIO: 1 – ♭3 – 5 – 7 – 9 – 11
CHORD FAMILY: min/Maj7

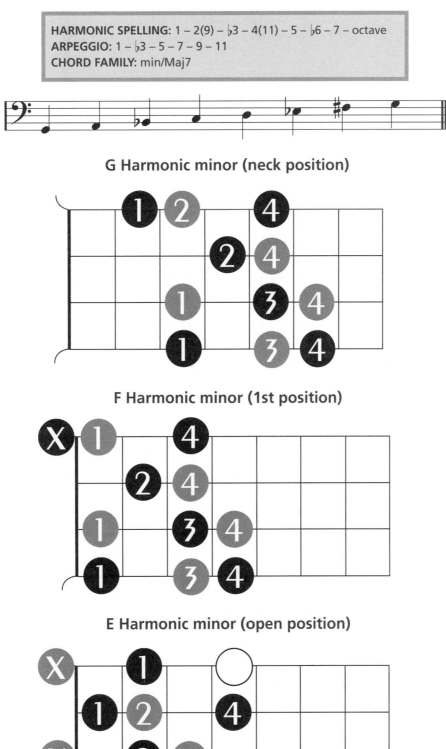

G Harmonic minor (neck position)

F Harmonic minor (1st position)

E Harmonic minor (open position)

PHRYGIAN #3 SCALE
5th mode of the HARMONIC MINOR scale
Also known as the SPANISH SCALE

HARMONIC SPELLING: 1 – ♭9 – 3 – 4(11) – 5 – ♭6 – ♭7 – octave
ARPEGGIO: 1 – 3 – 5 – ♭7 – ♭9 – 11
CHORD FAMILY: Dom7♭9
NOTE: Can be played on the V chord of a minor II–V–I.

G Phrygian #3 (neck position)

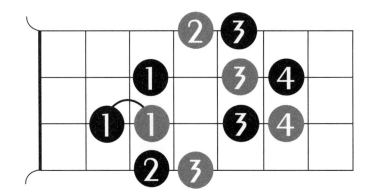

F Phrygian #3 (1st position)

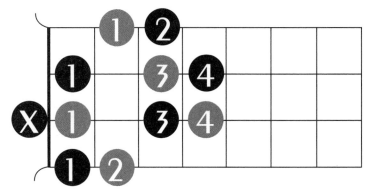

E Phrygian #3 (open position)

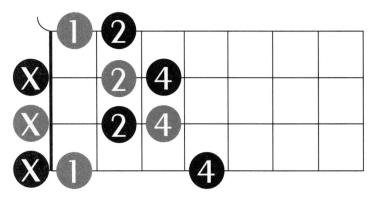

3.4
SYMMETRICAL SCALES

CHROMATIC SCALE
Symmetrical pattern: semitones

G Chromatic (neck position)

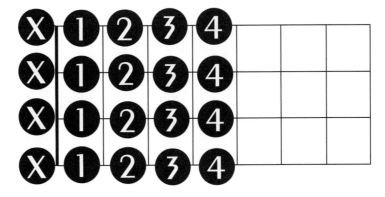

E Chromatic (open position)

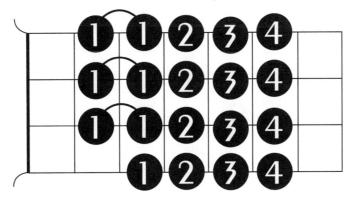

WHOLE TONE SCALE

Symmetrical pattern: whole tones

The whole tone scale is a six-note scale

HARMONIC SPELLING: 1 – 2(9) – 3 – #4(#11) – #5 – ♭7 – octave
ARPEGGIO: 1 – 3 – #5 – ♭7
CHORD FAMILY: Aug7, Dom7(#5,#11)
CHORD PROGRESSION: Can be used as a V chord in a major cadence.

G Whole tone (neck position)

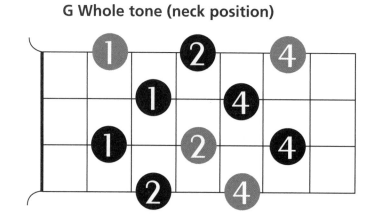

F Whole tone (1st position)

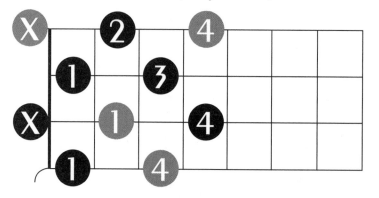

E Whole tone (open position)

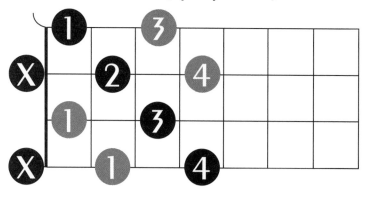

DIMINISHED SCALE

Symmetrical pattern: whole tone – semitone

The diminished scale is an eight-note scale

HARMONIC SPELLING: 1 – 2(9) – b3 – 4(11) – ♭5 – ♭6(♭13) – ♭♭7 – 7 – octave
ARPEGGIO: 1 – ♭3 – ♭5 – ♭♭7
CHORD FAMILY: dim7

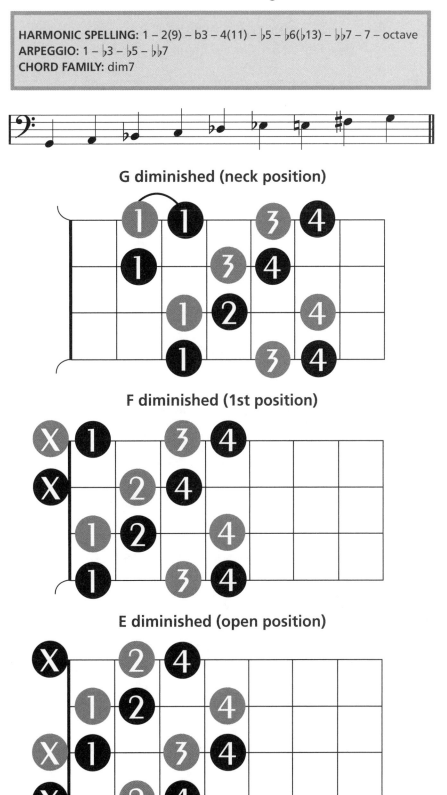

G diminished (neck position)

F diminished (1st position)

E diminished (open position)

THE DIMINISHED BLUES SCALE

Also known as
The HALF-STEP / WHOLE-STEP DIMINISHED
or
The 8 NOTE DOMINANT SCALE
Symmetrical pattern: semitone – whole tone

HARMONIC SPELLING: 1 – (♭9) – (#9) – 3 – #4 (#11) – 5 – 6 – ♭7 – octave
CHORD FAMILY: Dom7 (♭5, ♭9, #9, #11)
NOTE: There is no #5.
SPELLING: Because this scale has 8 notes, an alphabet note (besides the root) has to be repeated in the spelling of the scale.
CHORD PROGRESSION: Can be used on the V chord of the II-V-I progression.

G Diminished Blues scale (neck position)

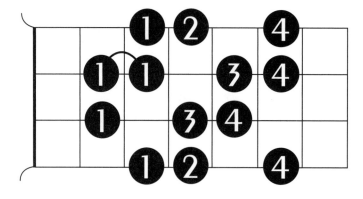

F Diminished Blues scale (1st position)

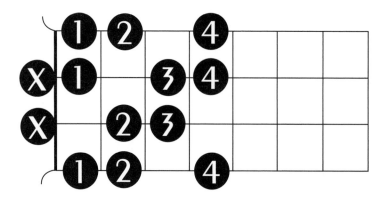

E Diminished Blues scale (open position)

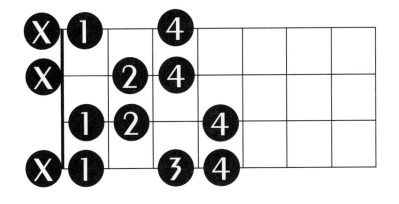

Optional Diminished Blues scale fingering

G Diminished Blues scale (neck position)

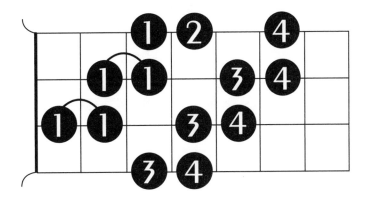

3.5
Modes generated by the ascending
MELODIC MINOR SCALE

MELODIC MINOR (ascending)
mode 1

> **HARMONIC SPELLING:** 1 – 2(9) – ♭3 – 4(11) – 5 – 6 – 7 – octave
> **ARPEGGIO:** 1 – ♭3 – 5 – 7 – 9 – 11
> **CHORD FAMILY:** min/Maj7
> **SHORTCUT TIP:** A shortcut to the melodic minor is to play a major scale and lower the 3rd to a minor 3rd.

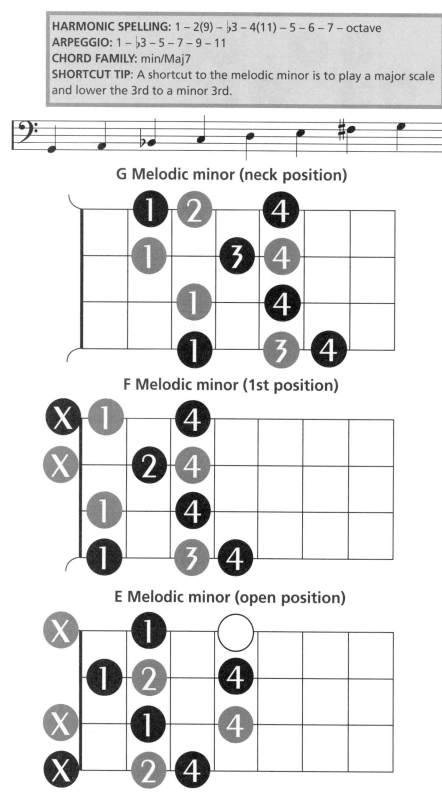

G Melodic minor (neck position)

F Melodic minor (1st position)

E Melodic minor (open position)

DORIAN ♭9 SCALE
mode 2

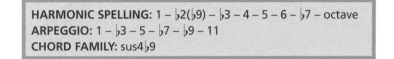

HARMONIC SPELLING: 1 – ♭2(♭9) – ♭3 – 4 – 5 – 6 – ♭7 – octave
ARPEGGIO: 1 – ♭3 – 5 – ♭7 – ♭9 – 11
CHORD FAMILY: sus4♭9

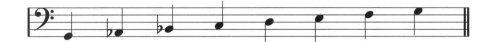

G Dorian ♭9 (neck position)

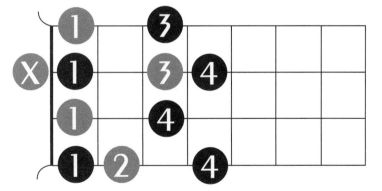

F Dorian ♭9 (1st position)

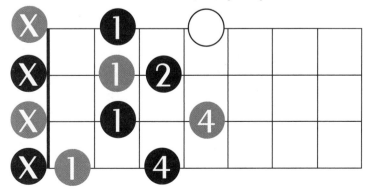

E Dorian ♭9 (open position)

LYDIAN AUGMENTED SCALE
mode 3

HARMONIC SPELLING: 1 – 2(9) – 3 – #4(#11) – #5 – 6 – 7 – octave
ARPEGGIO: 1 – 3 – #5 – 7 – 9 – #11
CHORD FAMILY: Maj7#5

G Lydian Augmented (neck position)

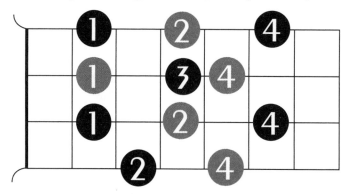

Lydian Augmented (1st position)

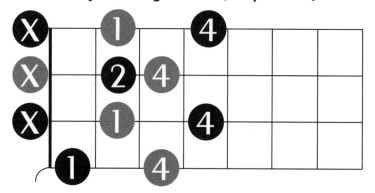

E Lydian Augmented (open position)

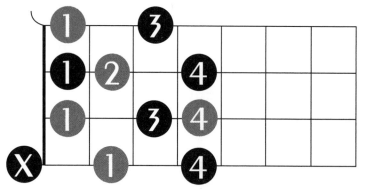

LYDIAN DOMINANT SCALE
Also known as the LYDIAN ♭7 or MIXOLYDIAN #4
mode 4

HARMONIC SPELLING: 1 – 2(9) – 3 – #4(#11) – 5 – 6 – ♭7 – octave
ARPEGGIO: 1 – 3 – 5 – ♭7 – 9 – #11
CHORD FAMILY: Dom7#11, Dom13

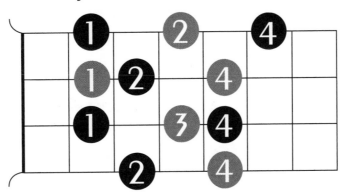

G Lydian Dominant (neck position)

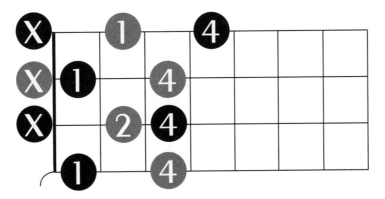

F Lydian Dominant (1st position)

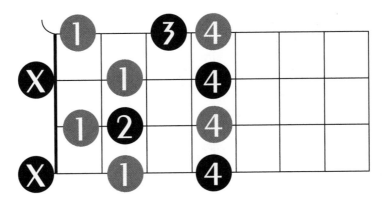

E Lydian Dominant (open position)

MIXOLYDIAN ♭13
mode 5

HARMONIC SPELLING: 1 –2(9) – 3 – 4 – 5 – ♭6(♭13) – ♭7 – octave
CHORD FAMILY: Dom7#5 Dom7♭13

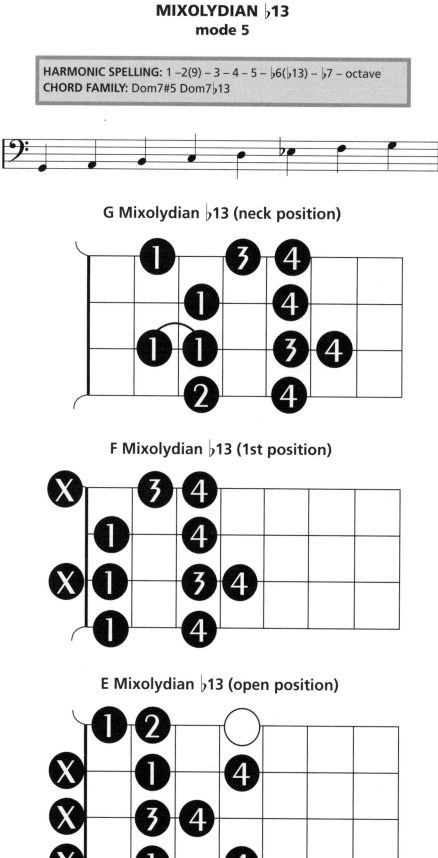

G Mixolydian ♭13 (neck position)

F Mixolydian ♭13 (1st position)

E Mixolydian ♭13 (open position)

LOCRIAN #2
mode 6

HARMONIC SPELLING: 1 – 2(9) – ♭3 – 4(11) – ♭5 – ♭6 – ♭7 – octave
ARPEGGIO: 1 – ♭3 – ♭5 – ♭7 – 9 – 11
CHORD FAMILY: min9♭5, (also written: Ø9)
NOTE: This is a half-diminished scale and chord with a natural 9.
CHORD PROGRESSION: The Locrian #2 scale can be used on the II chord of a minor II–V–I progression.

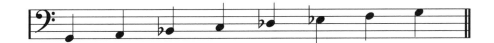

G Locrian #2 (neck position)

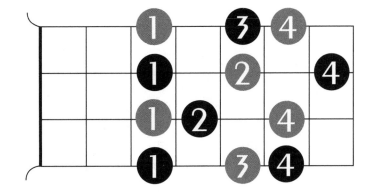

E Locrian #2 (open position)

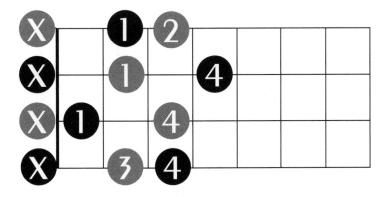

ALTERED SCALE
mode 7
Also known as THE SUPER LOCRIAN or the
DIMINISHED WHOLE-TONE SCALE

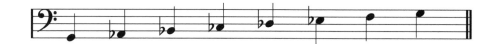

SCALE: 1 – ♭2 – ♭3 – ♭4 – ♭5 – ♭6 – ♭7 – octave
HARMONIC SPELLING: 1 – (♭9) – (#9) – 3 – #4(#11) – #5 – ♭7 – octave
CHORD FAMILY: Dominant chords which have altered 5ths and 9ths, i.e. (♭5/♭9, ♭5/#9, #5/♭9, #5/#9). Also known as an altered dominant chord, written C7 alt.
CHORD PROGRESSION: This scale can be used on the V chord of a minor II–V–I progression.

G Altered (neck position)

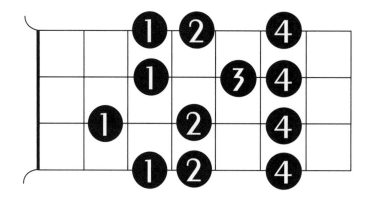

E Altered (open position)

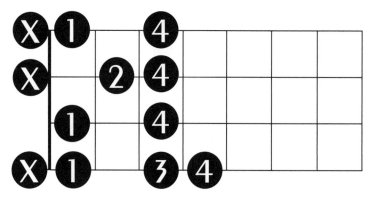

Optional ALTERED SCALE fingering

G Altered (neck position)

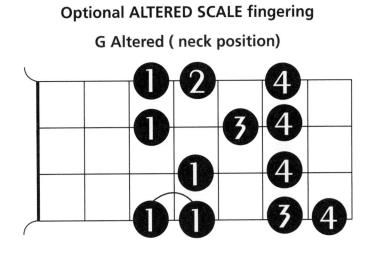

The HORIZONTAL connection of the MELODIC MINOR MODES

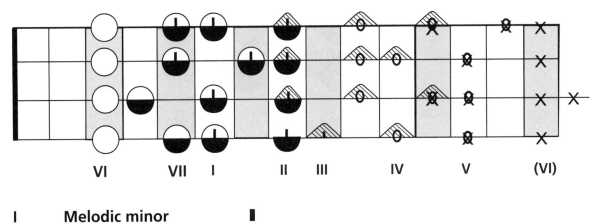

VI   VII   I   II   III   IV   V   (VI)

I	Melodic minor
II	Dorian ♭9
III	Lydian +
IV	Lydian ♭7
V	Mixolydian ♭6
VI	Locrian #2
VII	Altered

3.6
BEBOP SCALES
Note: There are more than these three.

BEBOP MAJOR SCALE

> **NOTE:** The chromatic passing note in the Bebop Major Scale is between the 5th and the 6th, indicated by the grey dot.

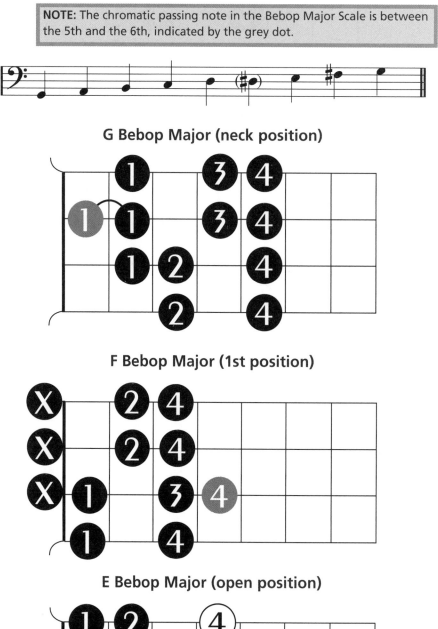

G Bebop Major (neck position)

F Bebop Major (1st position)

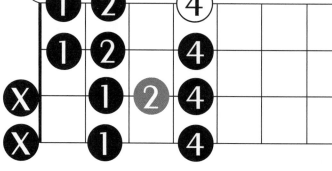

E Bebop Major (open position)

BEBOP DORIAN SCALE

NOTE: The chromatic passing note in the Bebop Dorian Scale is between the 3rd and the 4th, indicated by the grey dot.

G Bebop Dorian (neck position)

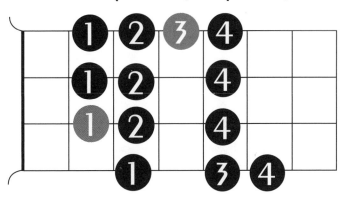

F Bebop Dorian (1st position)

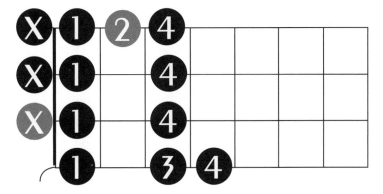

E Bebop Dorian (open position)

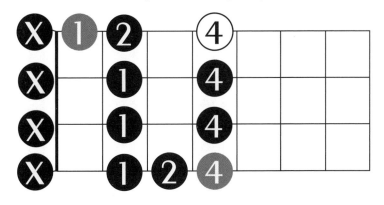

BEBOP MIXOLYDIAN SCALE

NOTE: The chromatic passing note in the Bebop Mixolydian Scale is between the 7th and the root, indicated by the grey dot.

G Bebop Mixolydian (neck position)

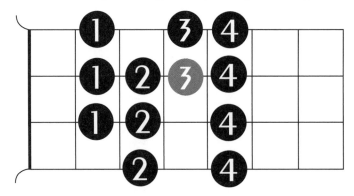

F Bebop Mixolydian (1st position)

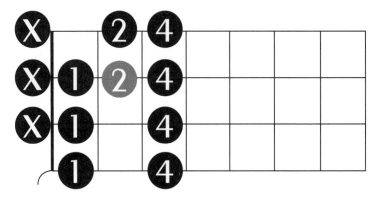

E Bebop Mixolydian (open position)

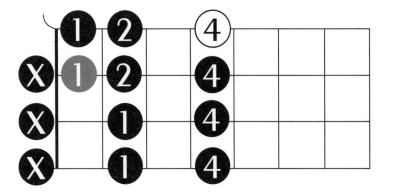

CHAPTER 4

2 OCTAVE SCALES & ARPEGGIOS
ON 4 STRINGS

Using two shapes
Shape 1: Vertical then horizontal on one string
Shape 2: Diagonal

4.1
The 7 modes generated by the MAJOR SCALE played over 2 octaves.

IONIAN (Major) SCALE
mode 1

HARMONIC SPELLING: 1 – 2(9) – 3 – 4 – 5 – 6 – 7 – octave	
CHORD FAMILY: Major chords, Maj7, Maj9, Maj6/9	
PASSING TONE: 4th	

G Major (shape 1)

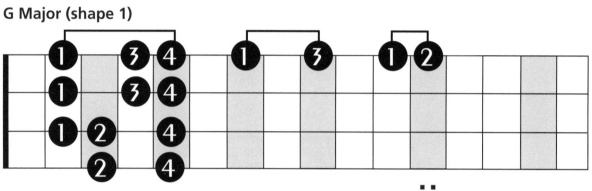

G Major (shape 2)

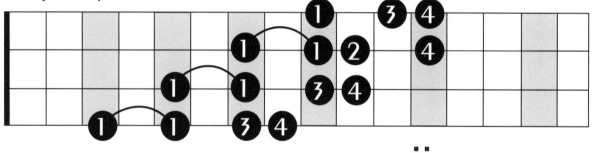

Maj7 arpeggio (1-3-5-7)

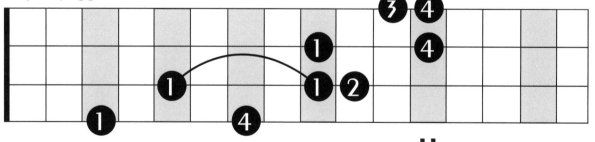

Maj13 arpeggio (1-3-5-7-9-11-13)

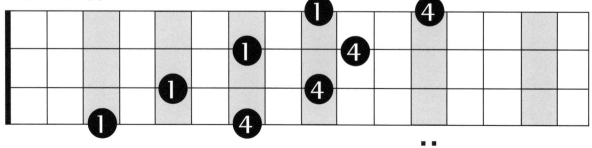

DORIAN SCALE
mode 2

HARMONIC SPELLING: 1 –2(9) – ♭3 – 4(11) – 5 – 6 (13)– ♭7 – octave
CHORD FAMILY: min6, min7, min9, min11, min13
CHORD PROGRESSION: The Dorian scale is used on minor I chords & the II chord of a
II–V–I progression .
SHORTCUT TIP: If we play any Aeolian scale and raise the 6th, we have the Dorian.

G Dorian (shape 1)

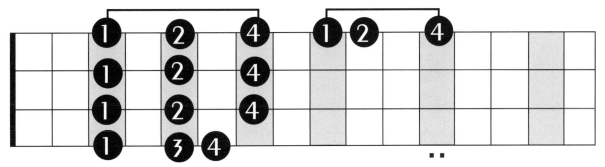

G Dorian (shape 2)

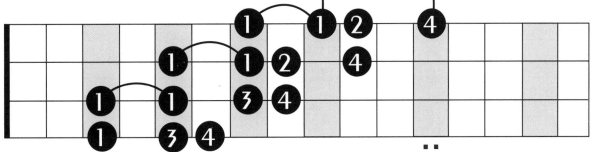

min7 arpeggio (1-♭3-5-♭7)

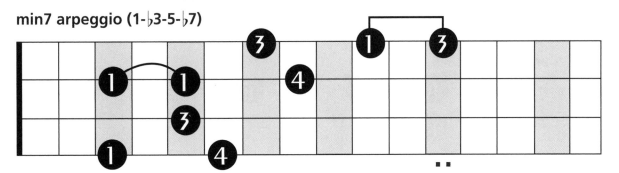

min13 arpeggio (1-♭3-5-♭7-9-11-13)

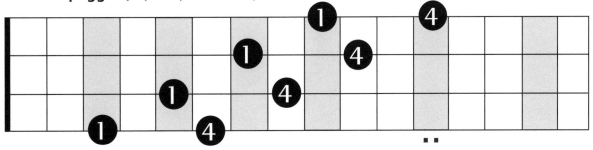

PHRYGIAN SCALE
mode 3

HARMONIC SPELLING: 1 – ♭2(♭9) – ♭3 – 4(11) – 5 – ♭6 (♭13) – ♭7 – octave
CHORD FAMILY: sus4♭9
NOTE: Notes most often played on a sus4♭9 chord are – root, ♭9, 4, 5, ♭7.
SHORTCUT TIP: Play an Aeolian scale and lower the 2nd note to get a Phrygian scale.

G Phrygian (shape 1)

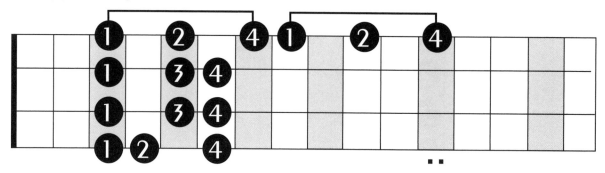

G Phrygian (shape 2)

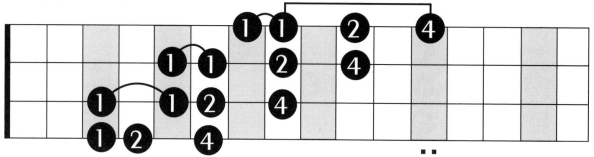

sus4♭9 arpeggio (1-♭9-4-5-♭7)

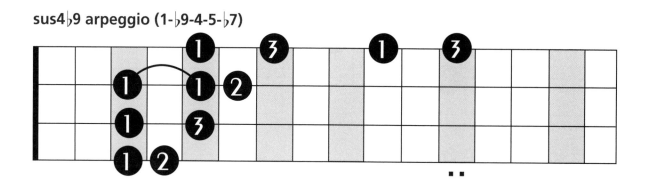

LYDIAN SCALE
mode 4

HARMONIC SPELLING: 1 – 2(9) – 3 – #4(#11) – 5 – 6(13) – 7 – octave
CHORD FAMILY: Maj, Maj 7, Maj7♭5, Maj7#11, Maj13#11

G Lydian (shape 1)

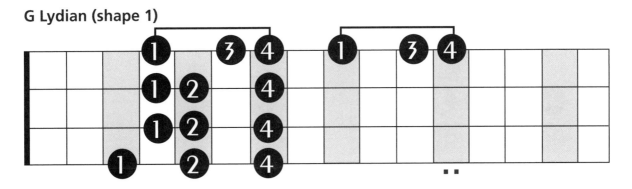

G Lydian (shape 2)

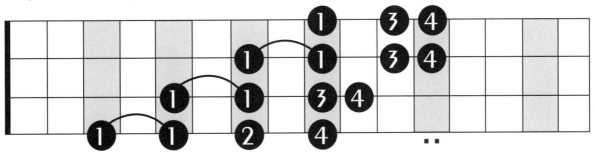

Maj7 arpeggios (1-3-5-7)

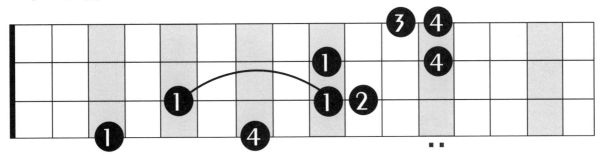

Maj13#11 arpeggios (1-3-5-7-9-#11-13)

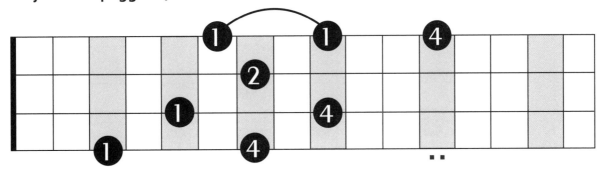

MIXOLYDIAN SCALE
mode 5

HARMONIC SPELLING: 1 – 2(9) – 3 – 4(11) – 5 – 6(13) – ♭7 – octave
CHORD FAMILY: Dom7, Dom9, Dom13, 7sus4
PASSING TONE (avoid note) is the 4th (excepting on a sus4 chord)
CHORD PROGRESSION: Can use the Mixolydian scale on the V7 chord of the II–V–I progression as well as on the Dom7 chords of the blues progression.

G Mixolydian (shape 1)

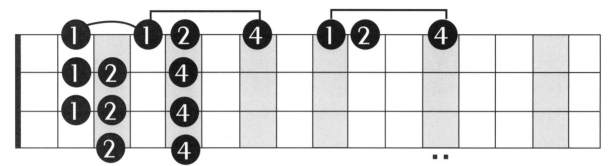

G Mixolydian (shape 2)

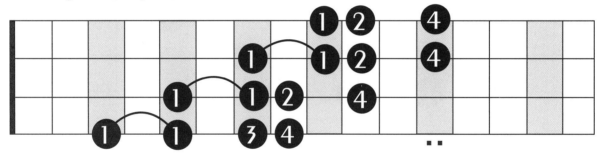

Dom7 arpeggio (1-3-5-♭7)

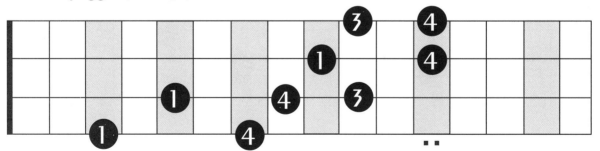

Dom13 arpeggio (1-3-5-♭7-9-11-13)

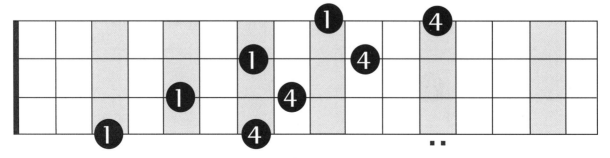

AEOLIAN (natural minor) SCALE
mode 6

The relative minor of the major scale with the same key signature.

> **HARMONIC SPELLING:** 1 – 2(9) – ♭3 – 4(11) – 5 – ♭6 – ♭7 – octave
> **CHORD FAMILY:** min7, min9, min♭6

G Aeolian (shape 1)

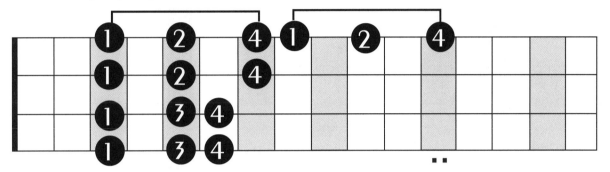

G Aeolian (shape 2)

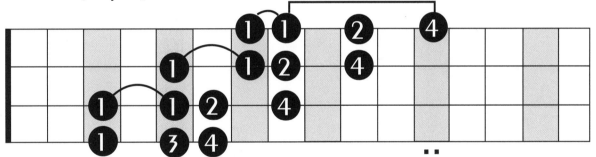

min7 arpeggio (1-♭3-5-♭7)

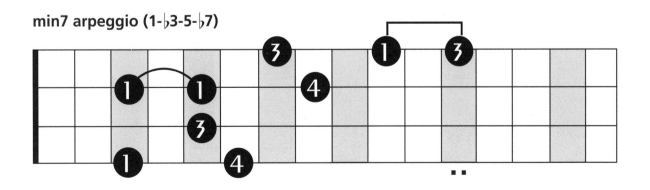

LOCRIAN SCALE
mode 7

> **HARMONIC SPELLING:** 1 – ♭2(♭9) – ♭3 – 4(11) – ♭5 – ♭6(♭13) – ♭7 – octave
> **CHORD FAMILY:** min7♭5 or Ø (called a 'half-diminished')
> **PASSING TONE** (avoid note) is the ♭9

G Locrian (shape 1)

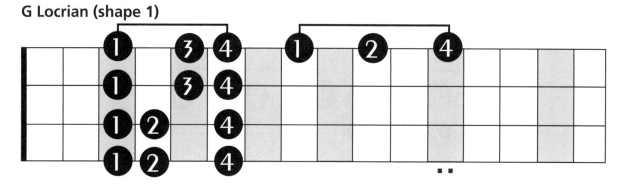

G Locrian (shape 2)

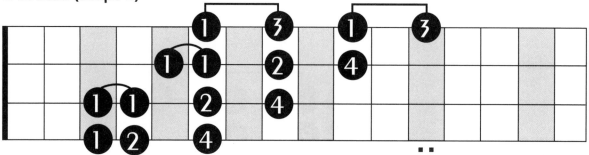

min7♭5 arpeggio (1-♭3-♭5-♭7)

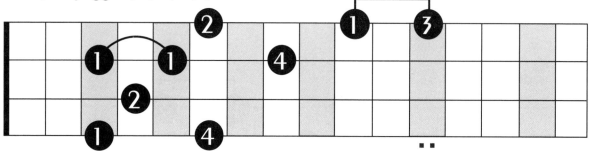

Half-dim (♭13♭9) arpeggio (1-♭3-♭5-♭7-♭9-11-♭13)

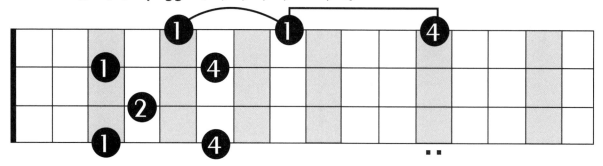

4.2
PENTATONIC and BLUES SCALES

MAJOR PENTATONIC SCALE

HARMONIC SPELLING: 1 – 2 – 3 – 5 – 6 – octave
CHORD FAMILY: Maj6/9, Maj7, Dom7
Note: If we were to play all the notes of this scale at the same time we would have a Maj6/9 chord.

G Major Pentatonic (shape 1)

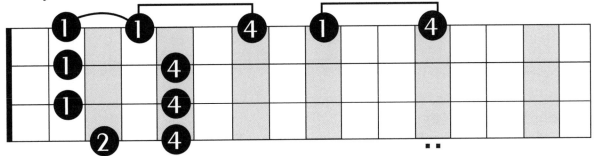

G Major Pentatonic (shape 2)

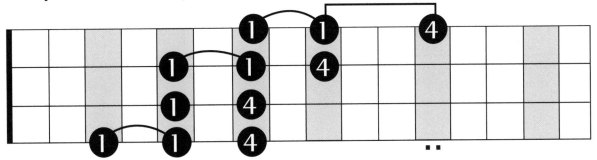

MINOR PENTATONIC

HARMONIC SPELLING: 1 – ♭3 – 4(11) – 5 – ♭7 – octave
CHORD FAMILY: min6, min7, min9, min11, min13

G minor Pentatonic (shape 1)

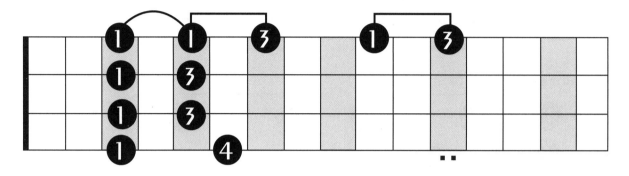

G minor Pentatonic (shape 2)

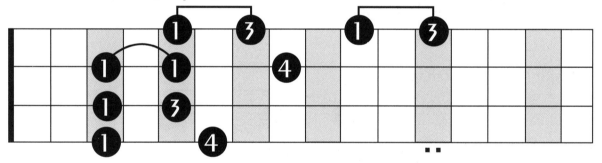

THE BLUES SCALE

HARMONIC SPELLING: 1 – ♭3 – 4 – #4 – 5 – ♭7 – octave
CHORD FAMILY: min7, Dom7 family chords

G Blues (shape 1)

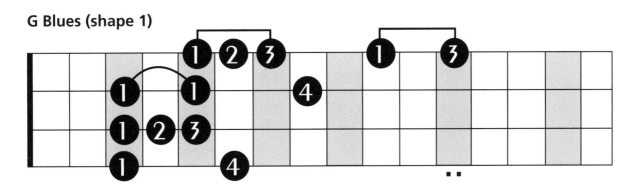

G Blues (shape 2)

4.3
HARMONIC MINOR

HARMONIC MINOR SCALE

> **HARMONIC SPELLING:** 1 – 2(9) – ♭3 – 4(11) – 5 – ♭6 – 7 – octave
> **CHORD FAMILY:** min/Maj7

G Harmonic minor

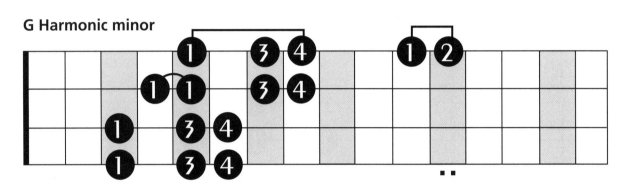

min/Maj7 arpeggio (1-♭3-5-7)

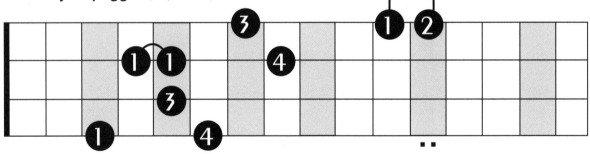

PHRYGIAN #3 SCALE

5th mode of the harmonic minor scale
Also known as the SPANISH SCALE

HARMONIC SPELLING: 1 – ♭2(♭9) – 3 – 4(11) – 5 – ♭6 – ♭7 – octave
CHORD FAMILY: Dom7♭9, Dom7(♭9#5)
NOTE: Can be played on the V chord of a minor II–V–I progression.

G Phrygian #3

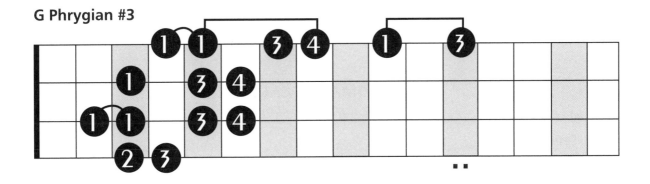

Arpeggio (1-3-5-♭7)

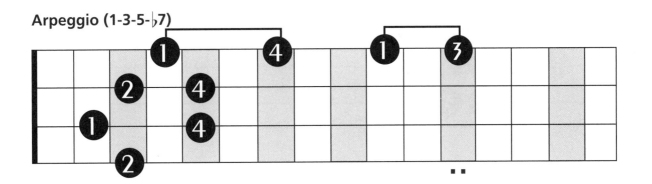

The Harmonic Minor and the Phrygian #3 connection

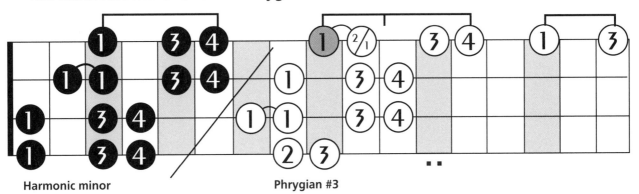

Harmonic minor   Phrygian #3

4.4
SYMMETRICAL SCALES
played over 2 octaves

CHROMATIC SCALE
Symmetrical pattern: semitones

G Chromatic

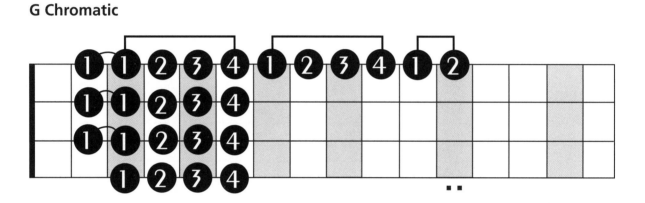

WHOLE TONE SCALE
Symmetrical pattern: whole tones
The whole-tone scale is a six-note scale

> **HARMONIC SPELLING:** 1 – 2(9) – 3 – #4(#11) – #5 – ♭7 – octave
> **CHORD FAMILY:** Aug7, Dom7(#5,#11)
> **CHORD PROGRESSION:** Can be used as a V chord in a major cadence.

G Whole tone (shape 1)

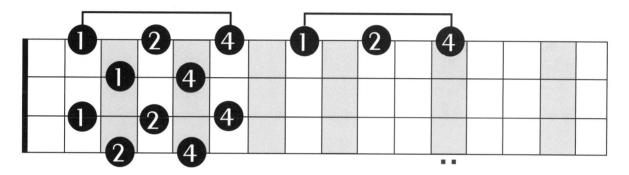

G Whole tone (shape 2)

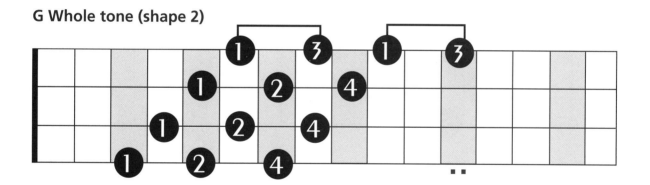

Dom7#5 arpeggio (1-3-#5-♭7)

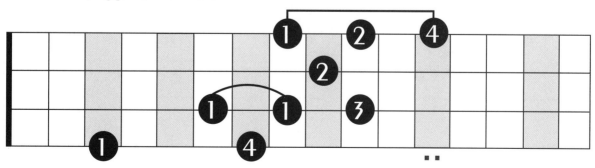

DIMINISHED SCALE

Symmetrical pattern: whole tone – semitone
The diminished scale is an eight-note scale

HARMONIC SPELLING: 1 – 2(9) – ♭3 – 4(11) – ♭5 – ♭6(♭13) – ♭♭7 – 7 – octave
CHORD FAMILY: dim7

G diminished (shape 1)

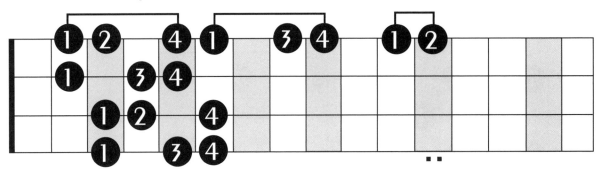

G diminished (shape 2)

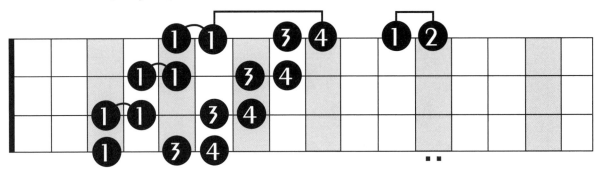

dim7 arpeggio (1-♭3-♭5-♭♭7)

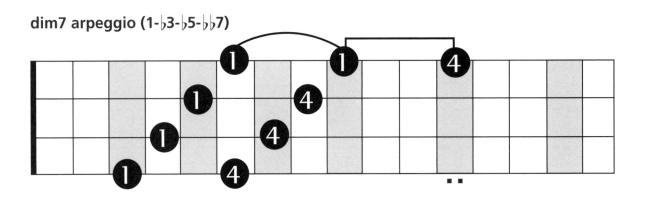

DIMINISHED BLUES SCALE
Also known as the
HALF-STEP / WHOLE-STEP DIMINISHED
or the 8 NOTE DOMINANT SCALE
Symmetrical pattern: semitone – whole tone

HARMONIC SPELLING: 1 – (♭9) – (#9) – 3 – #4 (#11) – 5 – 6 – ♭7 – octave
CHORD FAMILY: Dom7 (♭5, ♭9, #9, #11)
NOTE: There is no #5.
SPELLING: Because this scale has 8 notes, an alphabet note (besides the root) has to be repeated in the spelling of the scale.
CHORD PROGRESSION: Can be used on the V chord of the II-V-I progression.

G diminished blues scale (shape 1)

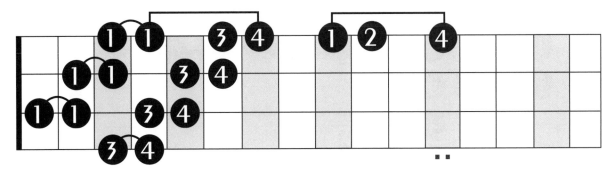

G diminished blues scale (shape 2)

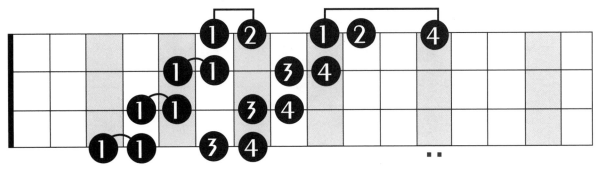

Dom7♭5 arpeggio (1-3-♭5-♭7)

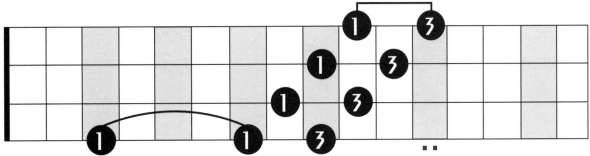

4.5
Modes generated by the ascending MELODIC MINOR SCALE played over 2 octaves

MELODIC MINOR *(ascending)*
mode 1

> **HARMONIC SPELLING:** 1 – 2(9) – ♭3 – 4(11) – 5 – 6 – 7 – octave
> **CHORD FAMILY:** min/Maj7
> **SHORTCUT TIP:** A shortcut to the Melodic minor is to play a major scale and lower the 3rd to a minor 3rd.

G Melodic minor (shape 1)

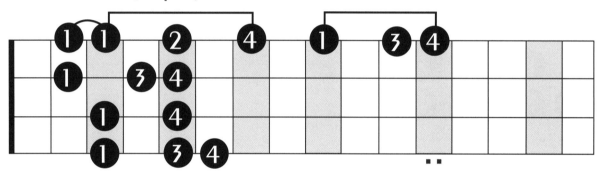

G Melodic minor (shape 2)

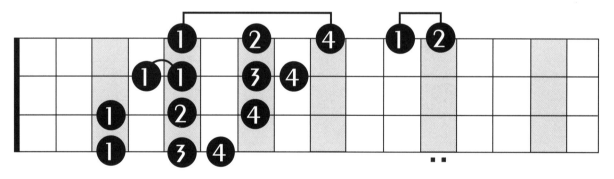

min/Maj7 arpeggio (1-♭3-5-7)

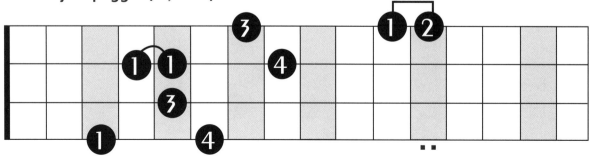

DORIAN ♭9 SCALE
mode 2

> **HARMONIC SPELLING:** 1 – ♭2(♭9) – ♭3 – 4 – 5 – 6 – ♭7 – octave
> **CHORD FAMILY:** sus4♭9

G Dorian ♭9 (shape 1)

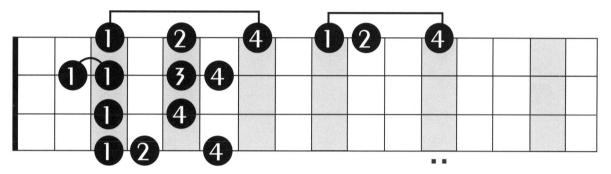

G Dorian ♭9 (shape 2)

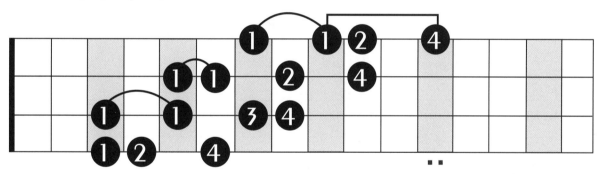

sus4♭9 arpeggio (1-♭9-4-5-♭7)

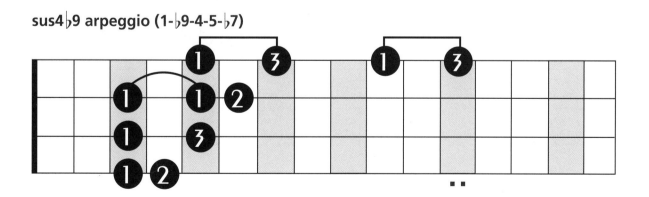

LYDIAN AUGMENTED SCALE
mode 3

HARMONIC SPELLING: 1 – 2(9) – 3 – #4(#11) – #5 – 6 – 7 – octave
CHORD FAMILY: Maj7#5
NOTE: Notice that the scale has a #11 which is not found in the chord.

G Lydian Augmented (shape 1)

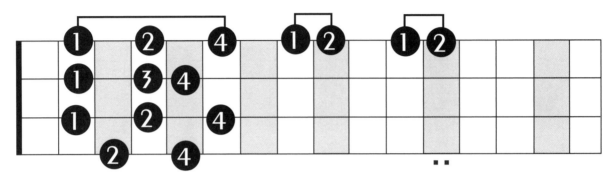

G Lydian Augmented (shape 2)

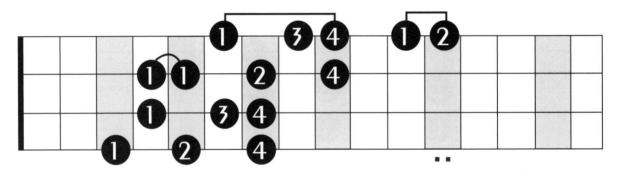

Maj7#5 arpeggio (1-3-#5-7)

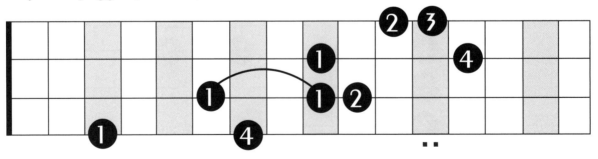

LYDIAN DOMINANT SCALE
mode 4

Also known as LYDIAN ♭7 SCALE or MIXOLYDIAN #4

> **HARMONIC SPELLING:** 1 –2(9) – 3 – #4(#11) – 5 – 6 – ♭7 – octave
> **CHORD FAMILY:** Dom7#11, Dom13

G Lydian Dominant (shape 1)

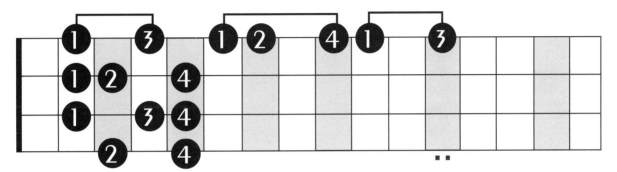

G Lydian Dominant (shape 2)

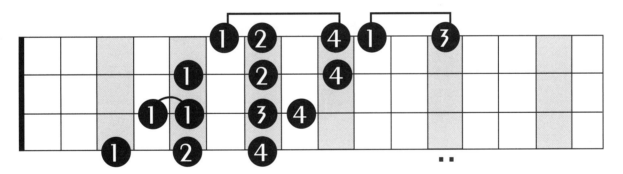

Dom7♭5 arpeggio (1-3-♭5-♭7)

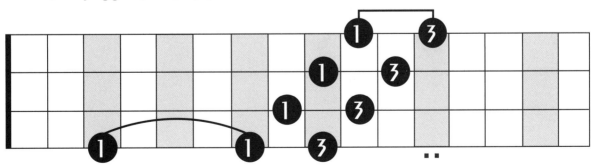

MIXOLYDIAN ♭13
mode 5

> **HARMONIC SPELLING:** 1 –2(9) – 3 – 4 – 5 – ♭6(♭13) – ♭7 – octave
> **CHORD FAMILY:** Dom7♭13, Dom7#5

G Mixolydian ♭13 (shape 1)

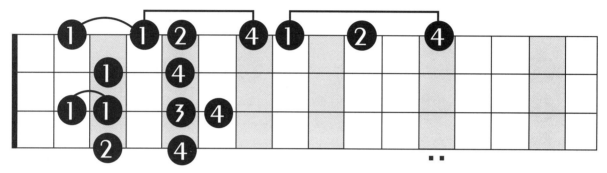

G Mixolydian ♭13 (shape 2)

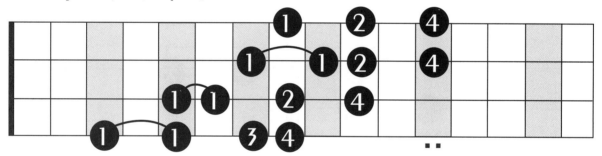

Dom7♭13 arpeggio (1-3-5-♭7-9-11-♭13)

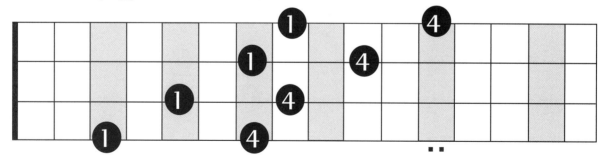

LOCRIAN #2
mode 6

HARMONIC SPELLING: 1 – 2(9) – ♭3 – 4(11) – ♭5 – ♭6 – ♭7 – octave
CHORD FAMILY: min9♭5 (also written: Ø9)
NOTE: This is a half-diminished scale and chord with a natural 9.
CHORD PROGRESSION: The Locrian #2 scale can be used on the II chord of a minor II–V–I progression.

G Locrian #2 (shape 1)

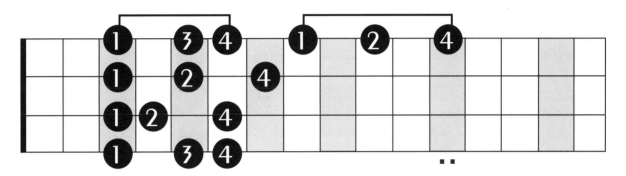

G Locrian #2 (shape 2)

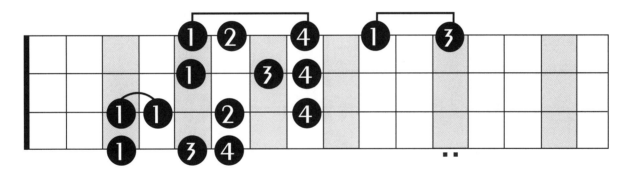

min7♭5 arpeggio (1-♭3-♭5-♭7)

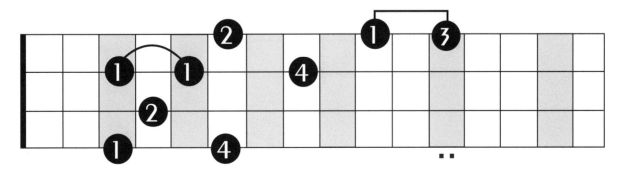

ALTERED SCALE
mode 7

Also known as THE SUPER LOCRIAN or the
DIMINISHED WHOLE-TONE SCALE

SCALE: 1 – ♭2 – ♭3 – ♭4 – ♭5 – ♭6 – ♭7 – octave.
HARMONIC SPELLING: 1 – (♭9) – (#9) – 3 – #4(#11) – #5 – ♭7 – octave.
CHORD FAMILY: Dominant chords which have altered 5ths and 9ths, i.e. (♭5/♭9, ♭5/#9, #5/♭9, #5/#9). Also known as an altered dominant chord, written C7alt.
CHORD PROGRESSION: This scale can be used on the V chord of a minor II–V–I progression.

G Altered (shape 1)

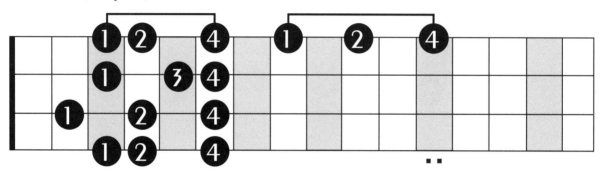

G Altered (shape 2)

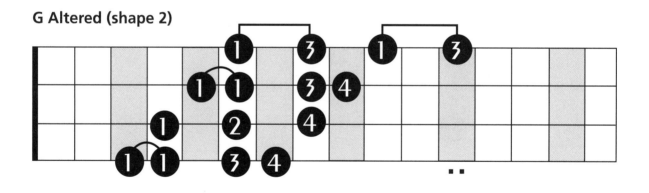

4.6
BEBOP SCALES
Note: There are more than these three.

BEBOP MAJOR SCALE

> **NOTE:** The chromatic passing note in the Bebop Major Scale is between the 5th and the 6th, as indicated by the grey dots.

G Bebop Major (shape 1)

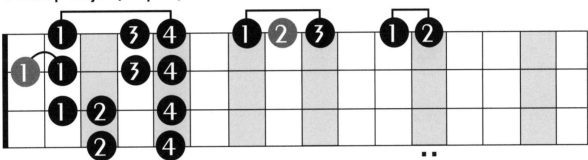

G Bebop Major (shape 2)

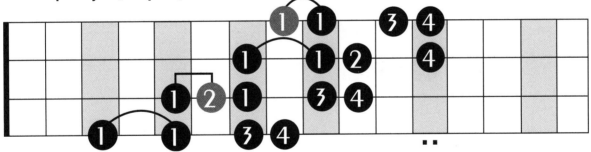

BEBOP DORIAN SCALE

NOTE: The chromatic passing note in the Bebop Dorian Scale is between the 3rd and the 4th, as indicated by the grey dots.

G Bebop Dorian (shape 1)

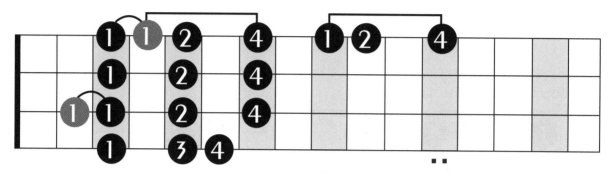

G Bebop Dorian (shape 2)

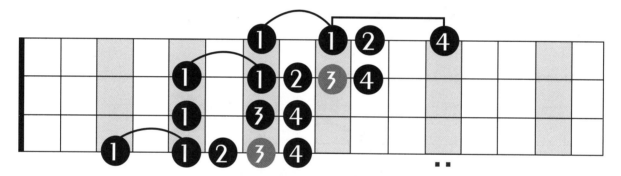

BEBOP MIXOLYDIAN SCALE

NOTE: The chromatic passing note in the Bebop Mixolydian Scale is between the 7th and the root, as indicated by the grey dots.

G Bebop Mixolydian (shape 1)

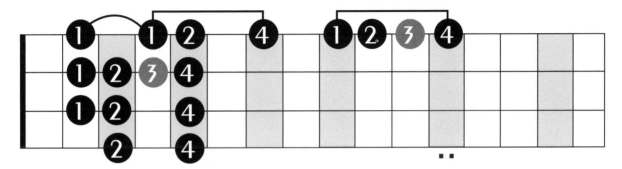

G Bebop Mixolydian (shape 2)

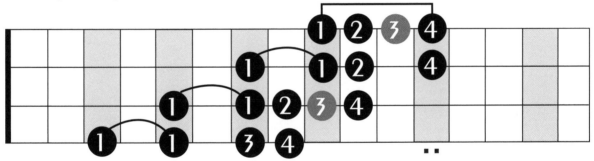

VERTICAL TWO OCTAVE SCALES ON FIVE STRINGS

5.1.
The 7 modes generated by the MAJOR SCALE

IONIAN (major) SCALE
mode 1

HARMONIC SPELLING: 1 – 2(9) – 3 – 4(11) – 5 – 6(13) – 7 – octave
ARPEGGIO: 1– 3 – 5 – 7 – 9 – 11 – 13
CHORD FAMILY: Major chords, Maj7, Maj9, Maj6/9
PASSING TONE: 4th

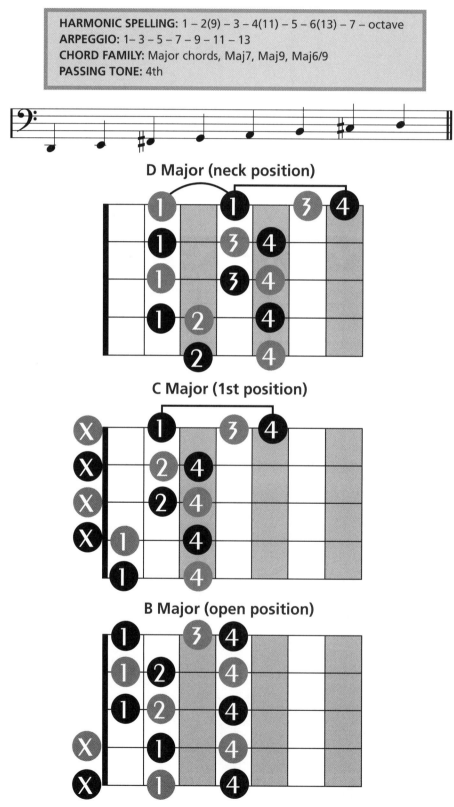

D Major (neck position)

C Major (1st position)

B Major (open position)

DORIAN SCALE
mode 2

HARMONIC SPELLING: 1 –2(9) – ♭3 – 4(11) – 5 – 6(13)– ♭7 – octave
ARPEGGIO: 1– ♭3 – 5 – ♭7 – 9 – 11 – 13
CHORD FAMILY: min6, min7, min9, min11, min13
CHORD PROGRESSION: The Dorian scale is used on minor I chords & the II chord of a II–V–I progression.
SHORTCUT TIP: If we play any Aeolian scale and raise the 6th, we have Dorian.

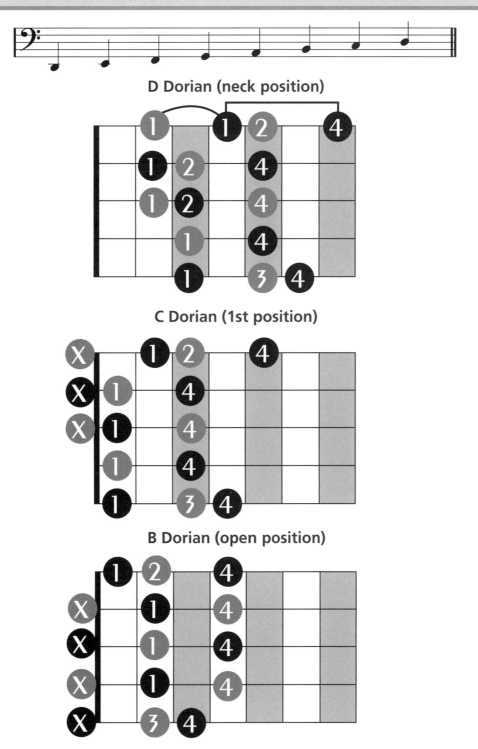

D Dorian (neck position)

C Dorian (1st position)

B Dorian (open position)

Optional DORIAN SCALE fingering

NOTE: This fingering is useful when shifting between the modes as well as playing certain scalar and intervallic patterns.

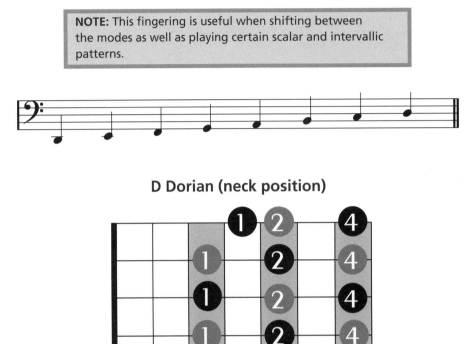

D Dorian (neck position)

PHRYGIAN SCALE
mode 3

HARMONIC SPELLING: 1 – ♭2(♭9) – ♭3 – 4(11) – 5 – ♭6(♭13) – ♭7 – octave
ARPEGGIO: 1– 3 – 5 – ♭7 – ♭9 – 11 – ♭13
CHORD FAMILY: sus4♭9
NOTE: Notes most often played on a sus4♭9 chord are – root, ♭9, 4, 5, ♭7.
SHORTCUT TIP: Play an Aeolian scale and lower the 2nd note to get a Phrygian scale.

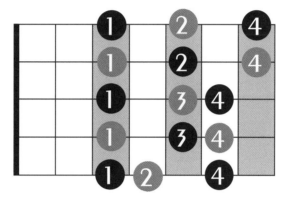

D Phrygian (neck position)

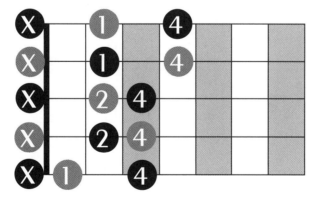

B Phrygian (open position)

LYDIAN SCALE
mode 4

HARMONIC SPELLING: 1 – 2(9) – 3 – #4(#11) – 5 – 6(13) – 7 – octave
ARPEGGIO: 1– 3 – 5 – 7 – 9 – #11 – 13
CHORD FAMILY: Maj, Maj7, Maj7♭5, Maj7#11, Maj13#11

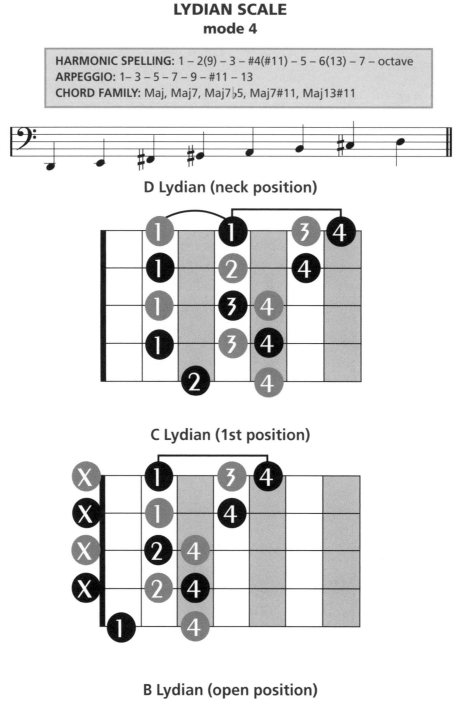

D Lydian (neck position)

C Lydian (1st position)

B Lydian (open position)

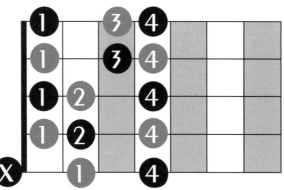

MIXOLYDIAN SCALE
mode 5

HARMONIC SPELLING: 1 – 2(9) – 3 – 4(11) – 5 – 6(13) – ♭7 – octave
ARPEGGIO: 1– 3 – 5 – ♭7 – 9 – 11 – 13
CHORD FAMILY: Dom7, Dom9, Dom13, 7sus4
PASSING TONE (avoid note) is the 4th (excepting on a sus4 chord)
CHORD PROGRESSION: Can use the Mixolydian scale on the V7 chord of the II–V–I progression as well as on the Dom7 chords of the blues progression.

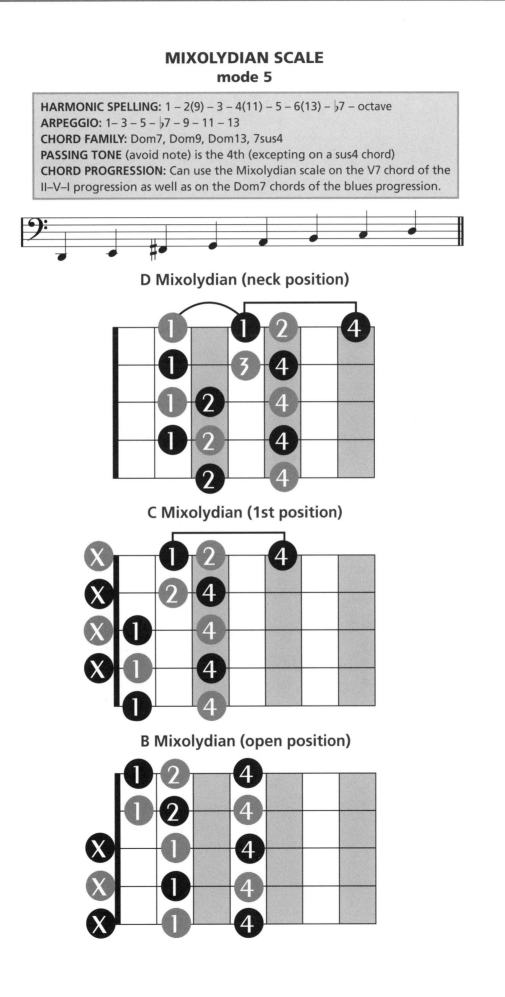

D Mixolydian (neck position)

C Mixolydian (1st position)

B Mixolydian (open position)

AEOLIAN (natural minor) SCALE
mode 6
The relative minor of the major scale with the same key signature.

HARMONIC SPELLING: 1 – 2(9) – ♭3 – 4(11) – 5 – ♭6(♭13) – ♭7 – octave
ARPEGGIO: 1 – ♭3 – 5 – ♭7 – 9 – 11 – ♭13
CHORD FAMILY: min7, min9, min♭6

D Aeolian (neck position)

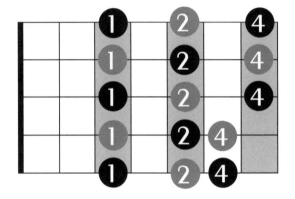

B Aeolian (1st position)

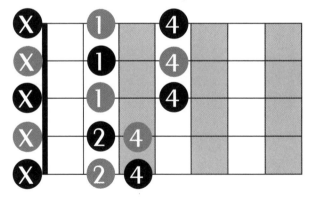

LOCRIAN SCALE
mode 7

HARMONIC SPELLING: 1 – ♭2(♭9) – ♭3 – 4(11) – ♭5 – ♭6(♭13) – ♭7 – octave
ARPEGGIO: 1– ♭3 – ♭5 – ♭7 – ♭9 – 11 – ♭13
CHORD FAMILY: min7♭5 or Ø (called a 'half-diminished`)
PASSING TONE (avoid note) is the ♭9

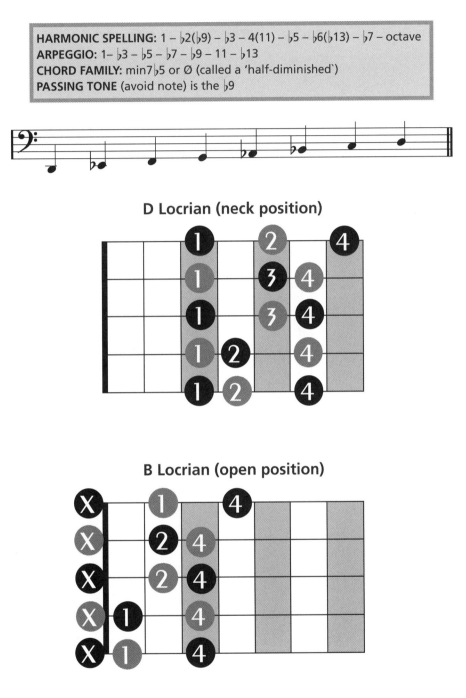

D Locrian (neck position)

B Locrian (open position)

5.2
PENTATONIC and BLUES SCALES

MAJOR PENTATONIC SCALE

HARMONIC SPELLING: 1 – 2 – 3 – 5 – 6 – octave
CHORD FAMILY: Maj6/9, Maj7, Dom7
NOTE: If we were to play all the notes of this scale at the same time we would have a Maj6/9 chord.

D Major Pentatonic (neck position)

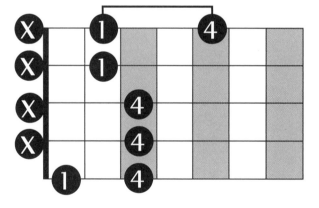

C Major Pentatonic (1st position)

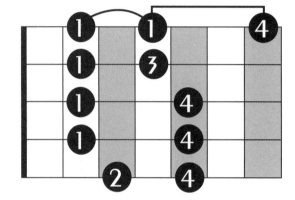

B Major Pentatonic (open position)

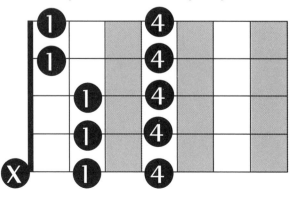

MINOR PENTATONIC

HARMONIC SPELLING: 1 – ♭3 – 4(11) – 5 – ♭7 – octave
CHORD FAMILY: min6, min7, min9, min11, min13

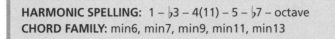

D Minor Pentatonic (neck position)

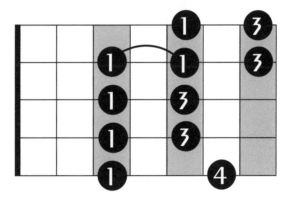

E Minor Pentatonic (open position)

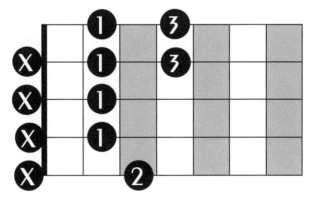

The 5 positions (modes) of the PENTATONIC SCALE
(On 5 strings)

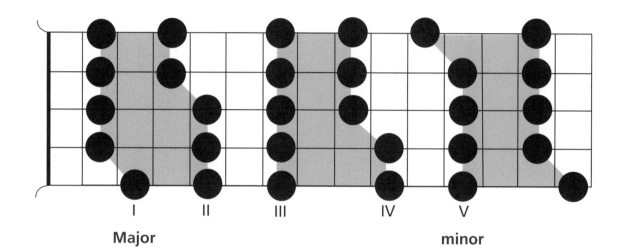

I II III IV V

Major   minor

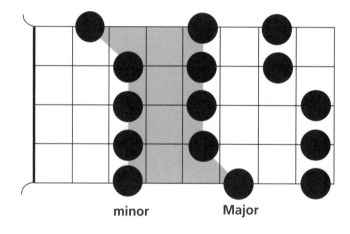

minor   Major

THE BLUES SCALE

HARMONIC SPELLING: 1 – ♭3 – 4 – #4 – 5 – ♭7 – octave
CHORD FAMILY: min7, Dom7 family chords

D Blues (neck position)

B Blues (open position)

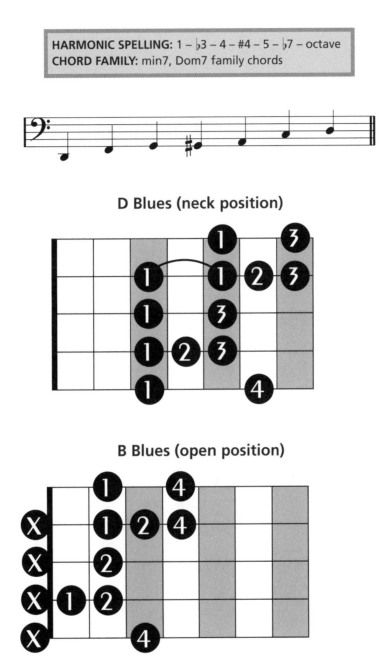

5.3
HARMONIC MINOR

HARMONIC MINOR SCALE

HARMONIC SPELLING: 1 – 2(9) – ♭3 – 4(11) – 5 – ♭6(♭13) – 7 – octave
ARPEGGIO: 1 – ♭3 – 5 – 7 – 9 – 11 – ♭13
CHORD FAMILY: min/Maj7

D Harmonic minor (neck position)

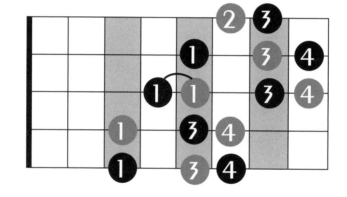

B Harmonic minor (open position)

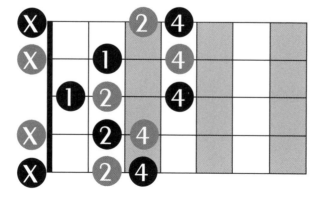

PHRYGIAN #3 SCALE
5th mode of the Harmonic Minor scale
Also known as the SPANISH SCALE

HARMONIC SPELLING: 1 – ♭2(♭9) – 3 – 4(11) – 5 – ♭6(♭13) – ♭7 – octave
ARPEGGIO: 1 – 3 – 5 – ♭7 – ♭9 – 11 – ♭13
CHORD FAMILY: Dom7♭9
NOTE: Can be played on the V chord of a minor II–V–I progression.

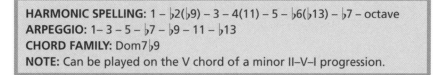

D Phrygian #3 (neck position)

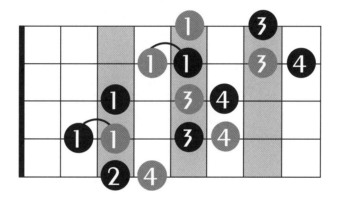

B Phrygian #3 (open position)

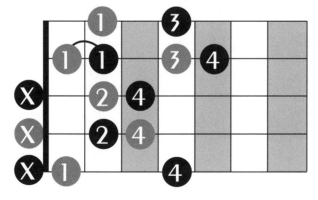

5.4
SYMMETRICAL SCALES

CHROMATIC SCALE
Symmetrical pattern: semitones

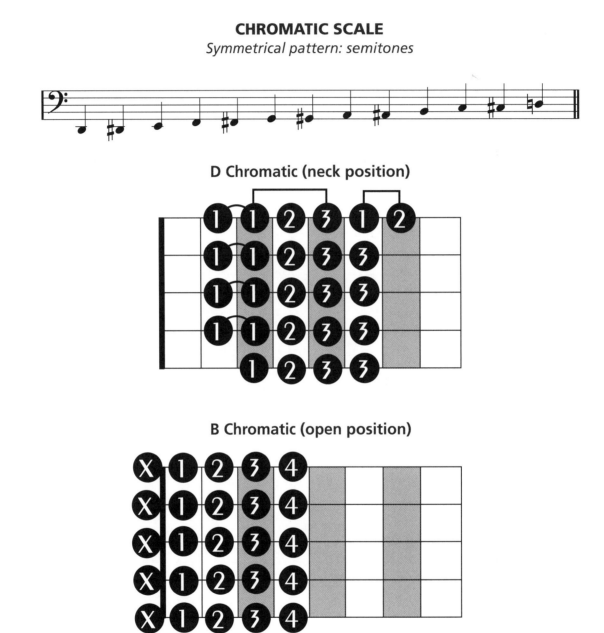

D Chromatic (neck position)

B Chromatic (open position)

Practice tip: Practice this two-octave chromatic scale (above) as 8th note triplets.

WHOLE-TONE SCALE
Symmetrical pattern: whole tones
The whole-tone scale is a six-note scale

HARMONIC SPELLING: 1 – 2(9) – 3 – #4(#11) – #5 – ♭7 – octave
CHORD FAMILY: Aug7, Dom7(#5,#11)
CHORD PROGRESSION: Can be used as a V chord in a major cadence.

D Whole-tone (neck position)

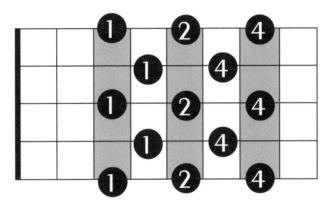

B Whole-tone (open position)

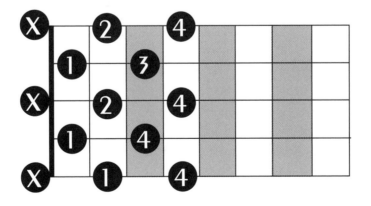

DIMINISHED SCALE

Symmetrical pattern: whole tone – semitone
The diminished scale is an eight-note scale

HARMONIC SPELLING: 1 – 2(9) – ♭3 – 4(11) – ♭5 – ♭6(♭13) – ♭♭7 – 7 – octave
ARPEGGIO: 1– ♭3 – ♭5 – ♭♭7
CHORD FAMILY: dim7

D Diminished (neck position)

C Diminished (1st position)

B Diminished (open position)

THE DIMINISHED BLUES SCALE
Symmetrical pattern: semitone – whole tone
Also known as
The HALF-STEP / WHOLE-STEP DIMINISHED
or
The 8-NOTE DOMINANT SCALE

HARMONIC SPELLING: 1 – (♭9) – (#9) – 3 – #4(#11) – 5 – 6 – ♭7 – octave
CHORD FAMILY: Dom7 (♭5, ♭9, #9, #11).
NOTE: There is no #5.
SPELLING: Because this scale has 8 notes, an alphabet note (besides the root) has to be repeated in the spelling of the scale.
CHORD PROGRESSION: Can be use on the V chord of a II-V-I progression.

D Diminished-blues scale (neck position)

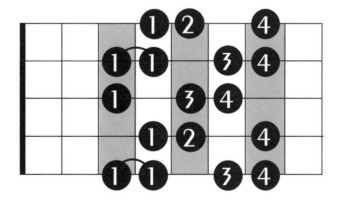

B Diminished-blues scale (open position)

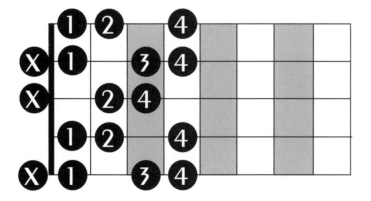

5.5
THE MODES GENERATED BY THE ASCENDING
MELODIC MINOR SCALE

MELODIC MINOR *(ascending)*
mode 1

HARMONIC SPELLING: 1 – 2(9) – ♭3 – 4(11) – 5 – 6 – 7 – octave
ARPEGGIO: 1– ♭3 – 5 – 7 – 9 – 11 – 13
CHORD FAMILY: min/Maj7
SHORTCUT TIP: A shortcut to the Melodic minor is to play a major scale and lower the 3rd to a minor 3rd.

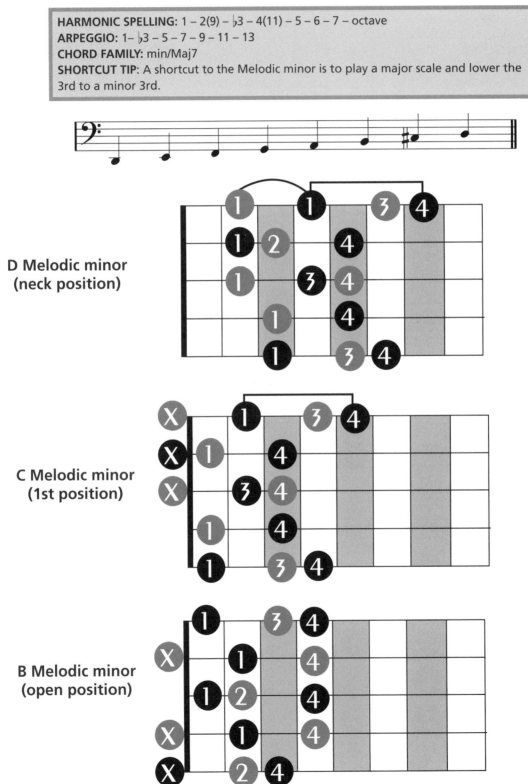

D Melodic minor
(neck position)

C Melodic minor
(1st position)

B Melodic minor
(open position)

DORIAN ♭9
mode 2

HARMONIC SPELLING: 1 – ♭2(♭9) – ♭3 – 4(11) – 5 – 6(13) – ♭7 – octave
ARPEGGIO: 1– ♭3 – 5 – ♭7 – ♭9 – 11 – 13
CHORD FAMILY: sus4♭9

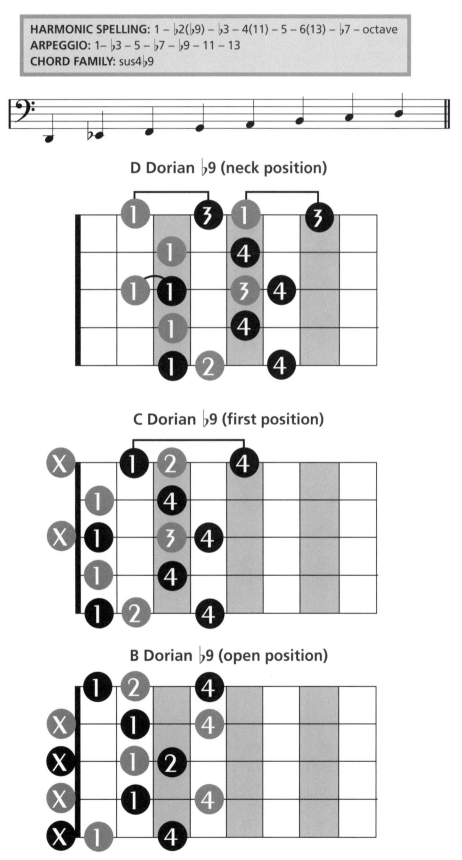

D Dorian ♭9 (neck position)

C Dorian ♭9 (first position)

B Dorian ♭9 (open position)

LYDIAN AUGMENTED SCALE
mode 3

HARMONIC SPELLING: 1 – 2(9) – 3 – #4(#11) – #5 – 6(13) – 7 – octave
ARPEGGIO: 1– 3 – #5 – 7 – 9 – #11 – 13
CHORD FAMILY: Maj7#5

C Lydian Augmented (1st position)

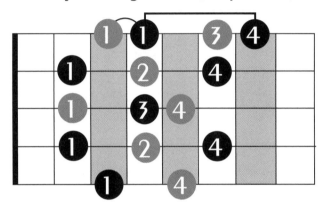

C Lydian Augmented (1st position)

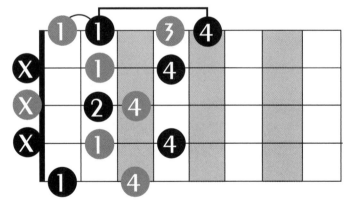

B Lydian Augmented (open position)

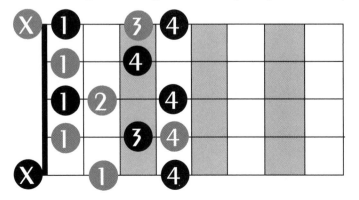

LYDIAN DOMINANT SCALE
mode 4
also known as the LYDIAN b7 or MIXOLYDIAN #4

HARMONIC SPELLING: 1 –2(9) – 3 – #4(#11) – 5 – 6 – ♭7 – octave
ARPEGGIO: 1– 3 – 5 – ♭7 – 9 – #11 – 13
CHORD FAMILY: Dom7#11, Dom13

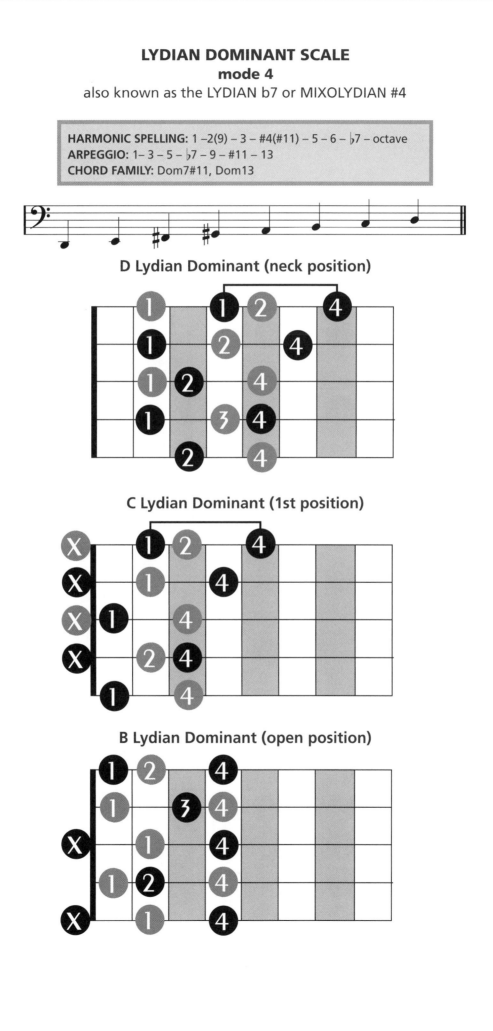

D Lydian Dominant (neck position)

C Lydian Dominant (1st position)

B Lydian Dominant (open position)

MIXOLYDIAN ♭13
mode 5

HARMONIC SPELLING: 1 –2(9) – 3 – 4 – 5 – ♭6(♭13) – ♭7 – octave
CHORD FAMILY: Dom7♭13, Dom7#5

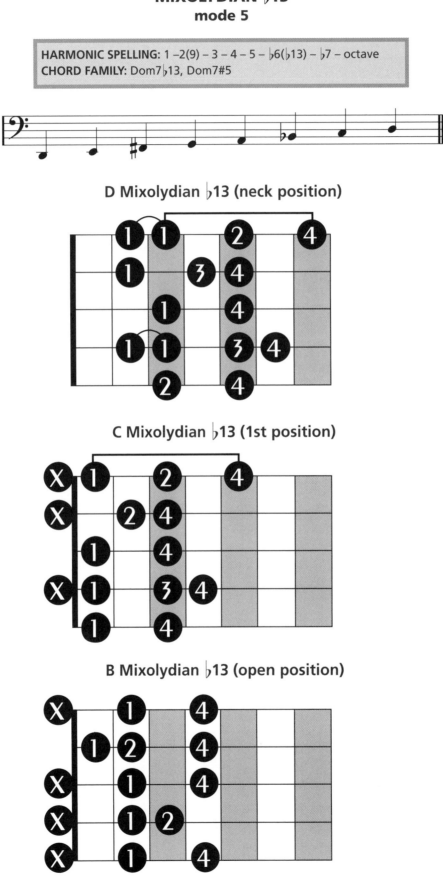

D Mixolydian ♭13 (neck position)

C Mixolydian ♭13 (1st position)

B Mixolydian ♭13 (open position)

LOCRIAN #2
mode 6

HARMONIC SPELLING: 1 – 2(9) – ♭3 – 4(11) – ♭5 – ♭6(♭13) – ♭7 – octave
ARPEGGIO: 1– ♭3 – ♭5 – ♭7 – 9 – 11 – ♭13
CHORD FAMILY: min9♭5, (also written: Ø9)
NOTE: This is a half-diminished scale and chord with a natural 9.
CHORD PROGRESSION: The Locrian #2 scale can be used on the II chord of a minor II–V–I progression.

D Locrian #2 (neck position)

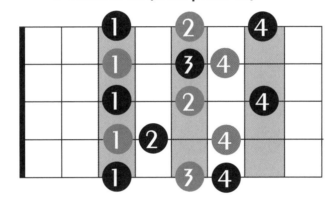

B Locrian #2 (open position)

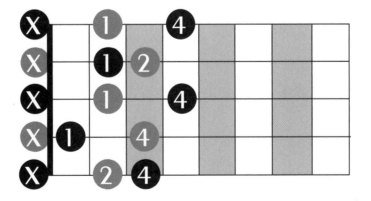

ALTERED SCALE
mode 7
Also known as the SUPER LOCRIAN SCALE

SCALE: 1 – ♭2 – ♭3 – ♭4 – ♭5 – ♭6 – ♭7 – octave
HARMONIC SPELLING: 1 – (♭9) – (#9) – 3 – #4(#11) – #5 – ♭7 – octave
CHORD FAMILY: Dominant chords which have altered 5ths and 9ths, i.e. (♭5/♭9, ♭5/#9, #5/♭9, #5/#9). Also known as an altered dominant chord, written C7alt.
CHORD PROGRESSION: This scale can be used on the V chord of a minor II–V–I progression.

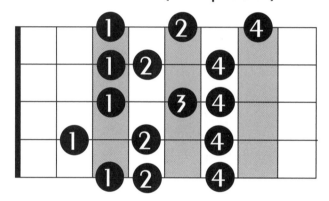

D Altered (neck position)

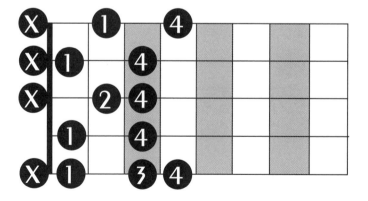

B Altered (open position)

Optional ALTERED SCALE Fingering

D Altered (neck position)

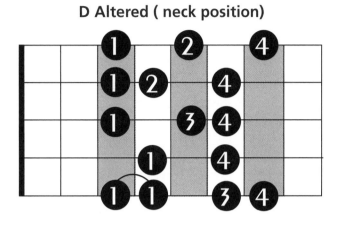

The HORIZONTAL connection of the MELODIC MINOR MODES
(5 strings)

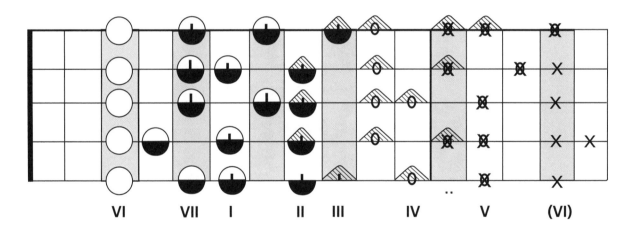

| VI | VII | I | II | III | IV | V | (VI) |

I	Melodic minor	▌
II	Dorian ♭9	
III	Lydian +	◿
IV	Lydian ♭7	O
V	Mixolydian ♭6	X
VI	Locrian #2	◯
VII	Altered	◖

5.6
BEBOP SCALES
Note: There are more than these three.

BEBOP (major) SCALE

> **NOTE:** The chromatic passing note in the Bebop Major Scale is between the 5th and the 6th, indicated by the grey dot.

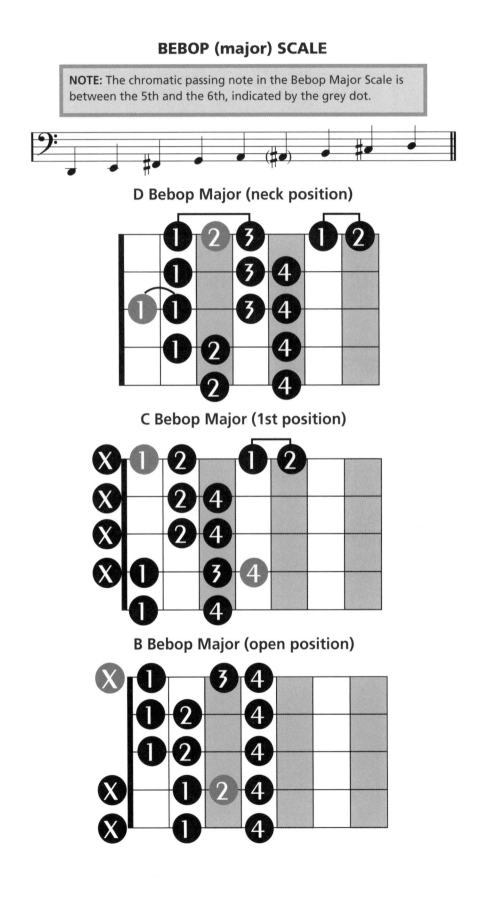

D Bebop Major (neck position)

C Bebop Major (1st position)

B Bebop Major (open position)

BEBOP DORIAN SCALE

NOTE: The chromatic passing note in the Bebop Dorian Scale is between the 3rd and the 4th, indicated by the grey dot.

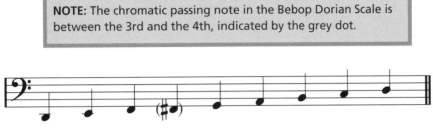

D Bebop Dorian (neck position)

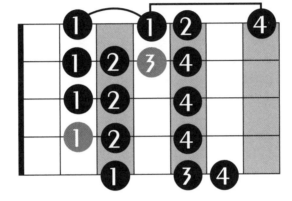

C Bebop Dorian (1st position)

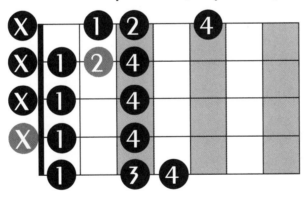

B Bebop Dorian (open position)

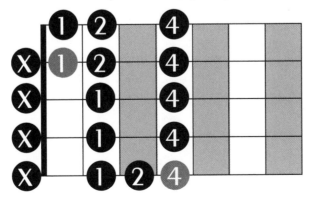

BEBOP MIXOLYDIAN SCALE

NOTE: The chromatic passing note in the Bebop Mixolydian Scale is between the 7th and the root, indicated by the grey dots.

D Bebop Mixolydian (neck position)

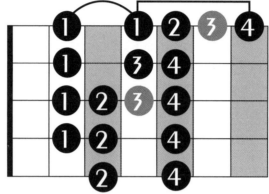

C Bebop Mixolydian (1st position)

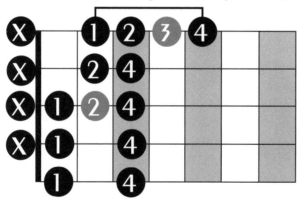

B Bebop Mixolydian (open position)

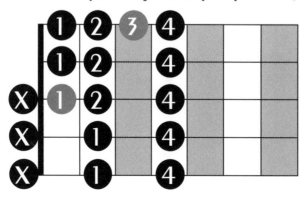

JAZZ THEORY CRASH COURSE

JAZZ THEORY CRASH COURSE

I have added a jazz theory section to this book not to imply that you should play jazz, but rather that you might have a deeper understanding of harmony and knowledge of how to apply the scales found in this book to your music. To fully understand and hear the information in this chapter, one should use the piano.

Diagram note: All vertical diagrams are constructed according to pitch, the highest note on top and the lowest note at the bottom.

6.1
INTERVALS

The distance in pitch from one note to another is called an INTERVAL. An interval consists of two notes; a lower and an upper note. Intervals are calculated by using the notes of the major scale as a reference. Each note of the major scale is given a position number from the TONIC up.

NOTE: The 1st note of a scale is called the TONIC, and the 1st note of a chord is called the ROOT.

Thus in the key of C major

C	8	*(Highest pitch)*
B	7	
A	6	
G	5	
F	4	
E	3	
D	2	
C	1	*(Lowest pitch)*

Intervals are always written as numbers, and chord positions* as Roman numerals.

Question: How does one work out an interval?

Answer: Build up a major scale from the lowest note of the interval, the lowest note being the tonic note of the major scale. Number the scale from the tonic note up, as in the above example. Thus, if the lowest note were F, the key and scale would be F Major. If the lowest note were E flat, the key and scale would be E flat major, and so on.

But before we can fully answer the above question we must first have an understanding of diatonic and altered diatonic intervals.

* chord positions will be looked at later on, on page 192.

DIATONIC

When the two notes that form the interval both belong to the same key and can be found in its scale, the interval is said to be diatonic. All intervals of the major scale are known as **MAJOR INTERVALS,** except the fourth, fifth and octave. These are described as **PERFECT INTERVALS**.

Here are the names of the diatonic intervals. For this example we are in the key of C. Note that each interval is worked out from the lowest note, which in this case is the note C.

C	Perfect 8th
B	Major 7th
A	Major 6th
G	Perfect 5th
F	Perfect 4th
E	Major 3rd
D	Major 2nd
C	TONIC

ALTERED DIATONIC INTERVALS.

If we alter the diatonic intervals up or down by a semitone, we get augmented, minor and diminished intervals. These are called altered diatonic intervals.

> **THE 3 NAMING RULES:**
>
> 1) If we raise a DIATONIC interval by a semitone we get an **AUGMENTED INTERVAL.**
> However, raising the 3rd simply becomes, and is, the perfect 4th. Therefore, one never uses the term, augmented 3rd. The same applies to the major 7th and the octave. One never uses the term augmented 7th.
>
> 2) If we lower a MAJOR interval by a semitone we get a **MINOR INTERVAL.**
>
> 3) If we lower a PERFECT interval by a semitone we get a **DIMINISHED INTERVAL.**
> However, lowering the perfect 4th by a semitone makes it a major third. Likewise, the 8th being lowered becomes, and is, the major 7th. Therefore in practice the only diminished interval we use is the diminished 5th.

Here are all the intervals (diatonic and altered diatonic) in the key of C.

		DIATONIC	ALTERED DIATONIC
8	C	OCTAVE	
7	B	MAJOR 7th	
	A# / B♭		Augmented 6th or minor 7th
6	A	MAJOR 6th	
	G# / A♭		Augmented 5th or minor 6th
5	G	PERFECT 5th	
	F# / G♭		Augmented 4th or diminished 5th
4	F	PERFECT 4th	
3	E	MAJOR 3rd	
	D# / E♭		Augmented 2nd or minor 3rd
2	D	MAJOR 2nd (Tone)	
	D♭		minor 2nd (semitone)
1	C	TONIC	

Now let's complete the answer.

Question: How does one work out an interval?
Answer:
   Step 1: Build up a major scale from the lowest note of the interval with the lowest note being the tonic note of the major scale.
   Step 2: Number the scale from the Tonic note up.
   Step 3: Place the upper note next to its coinciding letter name.
   Step 4: Analyse the note to see if it is the same, or has been raised or lowered by a semitone.

Example.

Question: "What is the interval between low E & upper C ?

Answer:
   Step 1: Treat the low E as the tonic note of E major.
   Step 2: Count up the diatonic intervals.
   Step 3: Place the upper note next to its coinciding letter. i.e. C next to C
   Step 4: Analyse the note to see if it is the same, or has been raises or lowered by a semitone.

Conclusion: In this case, the Major 6th has been lowered by a semitone, C# to C, therefore the interval is a minor 6th.

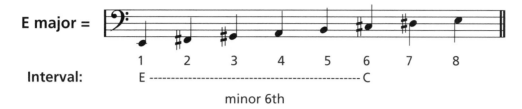

E major =

Interval: E --- C

minor 6th

DIATONIC SLANG

Musicians usually only use the numbers and not the words when talking about diatonic intervals. For example "play a 2nd", "play a 4th", "play a 5th", "play a 6th", except for MAJOR 3rd and MAJOR 7th.
"Play a major 3rd and a major 7th".

ALTERED DIATONIC SLANG

Minor 7th is sometimes referred to as "the 7th". Augmented notes are sometimes referred to as "sharp" and diminished as "flat". For example, "play a flat 5", or "play a sharp 9".

6.2
CHORDS

Jazz chords are usually made up of 7th chord harmonies and higher. But first let's look at the simple triad on which the 7th and other chords are built.

TRIADS

If you take the tonic, the third and the fifth degree of a major scale, 1 – 3 – 5 and stack them on top of each other, we have a major triad.

For example:
(C – E – G) stacked from the C up, would be a C Major triad.
By altering the diatonic intervals of this triad we get other different sounding triads. Here are the five triads that, besides being played as they are, also serve as foundation triads for many chords.

        1. Major: 1 – 3 – 5 (Happy sound)
        2. Minor: 1 – ♭3 – 5 (Sad sound)
        3. Diminished: 1 – ♭3 – ♭5
        4. Augmented: 1 – 3 – #5
        5. Suspended 4th: 1 – 4 – 5

Now let's add the 7th interval.

SEVENTH CHORDS and UP

Basically there are five different categories of 7th chords:

        1. Major 7th: 1 – 3 – 5 – 7
        2. Dominant 7th: 1 – 3 – 5 – ♭7
        3. Minor 7th: 1 – ♭3 – 5 – ♭7
        4. Half-diminished: 1 – ♭3 – ♭5 – ♭7
        5. Diminished 7th: 1 – ♭3 – ♭5 – ♭♭7

Question: Why is a "half-diminished" called that?
Answer: The diminished 7th chord is built up in intervals of minor 3rds. The half-diminished chord has a major 3rd interval between its last two notes, therefore it's not a full diminished.

Besides 7th chords there are a lot of other very interesting sounding chords. We can alter the perfect 5th or substitute the 3rd of the chord with the 4th or the 2nd, or the 7th with the 6th, and use the UPPER EXTENSIONS *(see next page) of certain chords and even alter them.

> **IMPORTANT NOTE:**
> All chords (excluding diminished) have a minor 7th unless indicated by the word 'major' or the symbol ∆. **THE WORD MAJOR ALWAYS REFERS TO THE 7th.**
> All chords (excluding diminished) have a major 3rd unless indicated by the word 'minor' or the symbol – or m. **THE WORD MINOR ALWAYS REFERS TO THE 3rd.**
> *Note: Half-diminished is a m7♭5*

For example:

C∆ indicates a ∆, therefore it has a major 7th

C7 has no indications therefore it has a major 3rd and a minor 7th

Cm7 indicates a 'm', therefore it has a minor 3rd and a minor 7th

Cm∆ indicates a 'm' and a ∆, therefore it has a minor 3rd with a major 7th.

THE UPPER EXTENSIONS

The upper extensions are notes that are found outside of the octave, but sometimes played within the octave.

C	D	E	F	G	A	B	C	D	E	F	G	A
1	2	3	4	5	6	7	8	9	10	11	12	13

- The 9th of a chord is the same note as the 2nd.
- The 11th of a chord is the same note as the 4th.
- The 13th of a chord is the same note as the 6th.

Question: Why not just call the 9th, 11th and 13th, the 2nd, 4th and 6th?

Answer: Playing those notes all at the same time makes no musical sense.

C	D	E	F	G	A	B
1	2	3	4	5	6	7

Now play these notes again, but this time take the 2nd, 4th & 6th notes out and play them up an octave.: (1 – 3 – 5 – 7) - (9 – 11 – 13). It makes better musical sense to build chords up in 3rds.

C		E		G		B		D		F		A

Chords are built from the root up to the highest interval. However, to understand what notes are in the chord one must look at it from the top note down. Just as the seventh floor of a building is supported from the ground floor up, if we tell someone to go to the seventh floor, it is not necessary to tell them to go to the 7, 6, 5, 4, 3, 2, 1, ground floor. We know that all those floors support the seventh floor. In the same way, it is not necessary to notate every interval of a chord, as the highest note is supported by the chord tones (notes of the chord) underneath it, so the chord will automatically include the chord tones below it. For example: the 9th chord will have the b7, 5, 3, and root, but is only notated as a 9th. The 13th chord will have the 11, 9, b7, 5, 3, and root, but is only notated as a 13th. If, however, we alter any of the diatonic notes besides the b7, the altered note has to be stated. For example C13#11.

Question: Why do we not go higher than a 13th?

Answer: Because there are only seven notes in a major scale or mode.

Question: What is the difference between C△#11 and C△♭5?

Cmajor7#11	
#11	F#
9	D
7	B
5	G
3	E
root	C

Cmajor7♭5	
7	B
♭5	G♭
3	E
1	C

Answer: Even though these chords have a similar sound, and the #11 (F#) and ♭5 (G♭) are the same enharmonic note, the C△#11 has the 5th (G) as well as the 9th. C△♭5 has none of these notes.

Question: Why is it favourable to sharpen the 11th?

Answer: One of the most dissonant intervals in music is not the semitone i.e. B and C. Play a G underneath the B and an E above the C and listen how the dissonance disappears on this Cmajor7 chord, in 2nd inversion (see page 183).

E
C
B
G

One of the most dissonant intervals is the ♭9 interval, e.g. C to the D♭ an octave above. In the key of E major, the ♭9 interval would be:

E major =

The interval of a ♭9 is E to F natural. Now let's go back to the key of C major and play a C△11 chord. Notice the ♭9 interval within the chord.

```
C – E – G – B – D – F
1   3   5   7   9   11

    E ------------------F
      ♭9 interval
```

The 11th of this chord is a ♭9 interval when played against the 3rd. i.e. E to F octave, and doesn't sound that pleasant. We can soften the sound of this interval by raising the 11 to a #11. On a minor chord, however, this interval does not exist, as the 3rd is flattened, therefore minor11 sounds great.

Note: a ♭9 interval sounds great on dominant 7th chords when the lowest note of the interval is the root such as C7♭9.

PASSING TONE (AVOID NOTES)

On the piano play a C major7 chord (root position)* with your left hand and play a C major scale with the right. Stopping on the F, the 4th note of the scale, while playing the C chord, creates the dissonant ♭9 interval. That is why the 4th is called the "avoid" note. However, if you played the 4th note within a run, such as a passing note, you would not notice the dissonance.

Because the dissonance it creates is sometimes desirable, a better word for an "avoid note" would be the "HANDLE WITH CARE" note, or "PASSING TONE".

* See page 183

POLYCHORDS and the shortcut to the upper extensions.

If on the keyboard we played a different chord with each hand at the same time, we would then have a polychord. A polychord is a chord over a chord. (*Note: A SLASH CHORD is a chord played over a single bass note*). To see the upper extensions on a 13#11 and minor13 quickly, we make use of the following polychords.

On a major13#11 notice that the upper extensions make a major triad (D triad) one tone up from the original major chord (C triad). Therefore if we played the polychord D over C and filled in which 7th we wanted i.e. dominant 7 or major 7 we would arrive at a 13#11 or Major 13#11 chord.

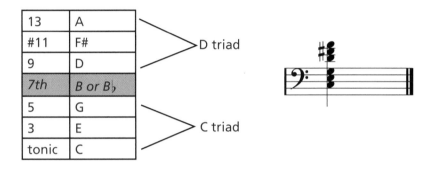

13	A
#11	F#
9	D
7th	B or B♭
5	G
3	E
tonic	C

D triad

C triad

On a minor 13th play a minor 7th with your left hand, move up a tone plus an octave and play that minor triad. Example Cm13 = the polychord Dm over Cm7.

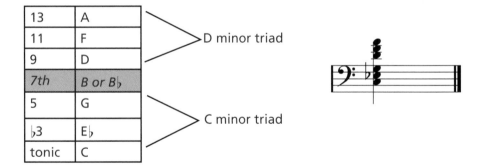

13	A
11	F
9	D
7th	B or B♭
5	G
♭3	E♭
tonic	C

D minor triad

C minor triad

RULE: PLAY THE SAME TYPE OF TRIAD THE LEFT HAND IS PLAYING, STARTING A TONE UP plus an OCTAVE.

IMPROV: Experiment playing the C7 chord and improvise using only the upper extensions, in other words the D triad.

INVERSIONS

If we were to take the root of a chord and place it on top, we would then have the 3rd of the chord on the bottom. This is known as 1st inversion. If we were to once again take the bottom note of the chord, the 3rd, and place it on top, we would then have the 5th of the chord on the bottom. This is known as 2nd inversion. If we were to once again take the bottom note of the chord, the 5th, and place it on top, we would then have the 7th of the chord on the bottom. This is known as 3rd inversion. Through all these inversions the name still stays the same because none of the notes have changed, just the order. If the order of the notes is not changed the chord is said to be in root position.

Example on a Cmajor 7 chord.

7	B
5	G
3	E
1	C

Root position

1	C
7	B
5	G
3	E

1st inversion.

3	E
1	C
7	B
5	G

2nd inversion

5	G
3	E
1	C
7	B

3rd inversion

THE DIMINISHED 7th CHORD INVERSIONS

The diminished chord is a symmetrical chord because it is built up in minor 3rds only. Lets look at the C diminished 7 chord with the tonic doubled on top.

Cdim7 = C – E♭ – G♭ – A – (C)

Now lets look at E♭dim7, G♭dim7 and Adim7.

E♭dim7 = E♭ – G♭ – A – C
G♭dim7 = G♭ – A – C – E♭
Adim7 = A – C – E♭ – G♭

Notice that all four of these chords have the same notes. Therefore, they are in theory all the same chord.
The same symmetrical inversions happen on D♭dim7 as well as Ddim7.
D♭dim7 = D♭ – E – G – B♭ – (D♭)
Ddim7 = D – F – A♭ – B – (D)

Conclusion: All 12 diminished 7th chords can be found in three chords.

THE AUGMENTED CHORD INVERSIONS

Like the diminished 7th chord, the augmented triad is a symmetrical chord because it consists of major 3rds only. Lets look at the C augmented with the tonic doubled on top.

C augmented. = C – E – G# – (C)

Now lets look at E and G# augmented,
E augmented = E – G# – C
G# augmented = G# – C – E

Notice that all three of these chords use the same notes, therefore they are all the same chord.

The same symmetrical inversions happen on D♭ augmented as well as D and E♭ augmented.

D♭ augmented = D♭ – F – A – (D♭)
D augmented = D – F# – A# – (D)
E♭ augmented = E♭ – G – B – (E♭)

Conclusion: All 12 augmented triads can be found in just four chords.

SLASH CHORDS

We saw earlier that a POLYCHORD is a chord over a chord. A SLASH CHORD is a chord played over a single bass note, for example F△7/G. Polychords are written using a horizontal line separating the upper and lower chords. A slash chord has a diagonal slash that separates the upper chord and the lower bass note. Slash chords make normal harmony more interesting, adding tension and release, and create nice bass line movement where the bassist plays other notes besides the root of the chord. Play these chords and then again as slash chords to hear the difference.

A	Dm	D7	Gm	A7	B♭△#11

A/C#	Dm	D/C	Gm/B♭	A7/C#	B♭△#11/ D

Note: Sometimes when the composer/arranger wants a slash chord, they sometimes write the word "bass" next to the bottom note just to make sure you understand that it is a slash chord.

Listen to these slash chords and notice how any major triad can be played over the same bass note and still sound good. Play and listen:

D♭maj/C Dmaj/C E♭maj/C Emaj/C Fmaj/C F#maj/C Gmaj/C A♭maj/C Amaj/C B♭maj/C Bmaj/C

IMPROV

To improvise over a slash chord one must analyse what the chord is when joined with the bottom note. For example: D♭maj over C is simply D♭maj7 with the 7th played on the bottom and you would use the D♭ major scale to play over this chord or starting on C, the Locrian. (The Locrian scale is explained in the section 6.8 MODES.) D over C could be a D7 chord with the 7th in the bass, or it could be a C chord with a 9 – ♭5 – 13 and then you could play a Lydian sound. (The Lydian scale is explained in the section 6.8 MODES.)

Slash chords are also used by composers to get the performer to play a certain inversion of a chord.
For example: C7#5#9 can also be written as Emaj7♭5/C.

When you have read, studied and understood chapter 6.8, "the 7 modes from the major scale", take a re-look at slash chords.

The re-look example:
The chords on the first eight bars of the jazz standard *On Green Dolphin Street.*

C△	C△	Cm7	Cm7	D7/C	D♭/C	C	C
C Major scale --------------		C Dorian --------------------		D Mixolydian	D♭ Lydian	C Major or C Lydian --------	

Question: Why choose D♭ Lydian & not D♭ Major scale over the D♭/C chord?

Answer: My ears told me.

6.3
THE CHORD CHART

All chord examples are in the key of C so that we can compare them to one another.

MAJOR

Lets start with a C major triad. In some cases, if the melody note is the tonic note (C), the major seventh will clash, so replacing the 7th with the 6th is sometimes a better option.

C6 = root–3–5–6 = C–E–G–A

To spice up the chord, add the ninth.

C6/9 = root–3–5–6–9 = C–E–G–A–D

If you only want the 9th (but no 7) you have to write "add" before the 9th.
C add 9, or also known as C2.

C2 = root–2–3–5 = C–D–E–G

Cadd9 = root–3–5–9 = C–E–G–D

(Without the word 'add', C9 would have a dominant 7).

MAJOR 7

Taking a major7 chord and adding a 9th we get CΔ9.

CΔ9 = root–3–5–7–9 = C–E–G–B–D

Because the 11 (the avoid note) clashes with the rest of the chord, we can sharpen it to make it sound nicer. This chord we call Cmajor7#11.

C7#11 = root–3–5–7–9–#11 = C–E–G–B–D–F#

#11 is the same note as #4. So without the 9 we have CΔ7#4. Usually with this chord we leave out the 5 as it clashes with the #4. We then call the #4 a ♭5 to keep the note names in 3rds. The common name for this chord is CΔ7♭5.

CΔ7b5 = root–3–♭5–7 = C–E–G♭–B

Note: When we finally analyze the modes in more detail, we will find that the scale that goes with this chord has a #4 and a 5th, so actually Δ7#4 is a more theoretically correct name.
If we sharpen the 5th of a Major 7 chord we get Δ7#5.

CΔ7#5 = root–3–#5–7 = C–E–G#–B

MINOR

Adding a 6th to a minor triad we get a minor 6 chord.

Cm6   =   root–♭3–5–6   =   C–E♭–G–A

Adding a 9th to a minor triad (without the 7th) we have Cm(add9). The 9th sounds nice when played down an octave as a 2nd.

Cm(add9)   =   root–(9)–♭3–5   =   C–D–E♭–G

Cm6/9   =   root–(9)–♭3–5–6   =   C–D–E♭–G–A

Cm♭6   =   root–♭3–5–♭6   =   C–E♭–G–A♭ = (A♭△7 in 1st inversion)

MINOR 7

On a minor7 chord when adding a 9th we get Cm9.

Cm9   =   root–♭3–5–♭7–9   =   C–E♭–G–B♭–D

Cm11   =   root–♭3–5–♭7–9–11   =   C–E♭–G–B♭–D–F

Cm13 = root–♭3–5–♭7–9–11–13 = C–E♭–G–B♭–D–F–A

Minor/MAJOR 7

If you put a Major 7 on top of a minor triad you get minor/Major 7.

Cm△7   =   root–♭3–5–7   =   C–E♭–G–B

DOMINANT 7

C9   =   root–3–5–♭7–9   =   C–E–G–B♭–D

Because the 11 (the avoid note) clashes with the rest of the chord, we can sharpen it to make it sound nicer. This chord we call C7#11.

C7#11   =   root–3–5–♭7–9–#11   =   C–E–G–B♭–D–F#

C13 = root–3–5–♭7–9–11–13   =   C–E–G–B♭–D–F–A

C13#11   =   root–3–5–♭7–9–#11–13   =   C–E–G–B♭–D–F#–A

DOMINANT 7 (ALTERED)

The dominant 7 chord has the most possibilities of altered notes. The notes altered are either the 5th or the 9th, or both.

C7b5   =   root–3–♭5–♭7   =   C–E–G♭–B♭

C7#5   =   root–3–#5–♭7   =   C–E–G#–B♭

This chord is also know as C7 augmented, written C7+.

C7b9   =   root–3–5–♭7–♭9   =   C–E–G–B♭–D♭

C7#9   =   root–3–5–♭7–#9   =   C–E–G–B♭–D#

These altered 5ths and 9ths can be used in various combinations.

For example:

C7♭5#9,   C7♭5♭9,   C7 5#9,   C7#5♭9.

If the composer leaves the decision up to the performer as to what 5ths and 9ths he wanted to alter, the composer would simply write "C7alt" on the chart. "C7alt" meaning C dominant 7 altered.

SUSPENDED DOMINANT 7

C7sus4	=	root–4–5–♭7	=	C–F–G–B♭

The 4 replaces 3

C9sus4	=	root–4–5–♭7–9	=	C–F–G–B♭–D

Csus2	=	root–2–5	=	C–D-G

The 2 replaces 3.

A "sus7" chord can also have an altered 9th.

C7sus♭9	=	root–4–5–♭7–♭9	=	C–F–G–B♭–D♭

(Playing the 9th an octave down on this chord sounds good.)

SUSPENDED MAJOR 7

A sus chord can also (if indicated) have a major 7 interval, and even a ♭5.

C△7sus4	=	root–4–5–7	=	C–F–G–B

C△7sus♭5	=	root–4–♭5–7	=	C–F–G♭–B

AUGMENTED

Lets start with the triad of C augmented, notated Caug or C+.

C+	=	root–3–#5	=	C–E–G#

We have already done augmented 7 (dominant alt.), but let's do it again.

C7+	=	root–3–#5–♭7	=	C–E–G#–B♭

We have already done augmented major 7, but let's do it again.

C△7+	=	root–3–#5–7	=	C–E–G#–B

HALF-DIMINISHED

Notated as m7♭5 or Ø.

CØ	=	root–♭3–♭5–♭7	=	C–E♭–G♭-B♭

In the half-diminished scale the 2nd note is a ♭9 and is the "avoid note." Rather raise it to the 9th.

CØ9	=	root–♭3–♭5–♭7–9	=	C–E♭–G♭–B♭-D

HALF-DIMINISHED SUS 4

Notated as CØsus4.

CØsus4 = root–4–♭5–♭7 = C–F–G♭-B♭

Note: CØsus4 is just another inversion of G♭Δ7-5.

DIMINISHED

Notated as dim or °.

C° = root–♭3–♭5 = C–E♭–G♭

DIMINISHED 7

Cdim7 = root–♭3–♭5–♭♭7 (6th) = C–E♭–G♭–A

Diminished/major 7 = diminished chord with a major 7 interval on top.

CdimΔ7 = root–♭3–♭5–6–7 = C–E♭–G♭–A–B

Note: CdimΔ7 is just another inversion of B7♭9.

OMIT 3

If you do not want the 3rd you notate it like this:

C(add9 / omit 3) = root–5–9 = C–G–D

C7(omit 3) = root–5–♭7 = C–G–B♭

C5 = Root–5 = C–G (Also known as a "Power chord".)

N.C. stands for "No Chord".

6.4
THE MYSTERY CHORD

How do we work out what name to give a chord from a group of notes, especially in contemporary music where there can be more than one name for this chord? Here is a system to derive the best choice — the most uncomplicated, easy to understand-at-a-glance chord.

THE MYSTERY CHORD ANALYSIS:

Chord names are derived from the building up of a chord starting on the root and going up using the uneven numbers (root-3-5-7-9-11-13) diatonically or altered, with the exception of the sus4 & sus2 replacing 3, or the 6th replacing the 7th.

When analyzing a chord, bearing in mind that chords can be written using different inversions, our first option should be to make the lowest note of the mystery chord the root, and the second option to treat the lowest note as the bass note of a mystery slash chord.

Step 1: Pick a note from the chord. Make that note the tonic of a major scale.
Step 2: Build up a full diatonic Major 13th chord from that note.
Step 3: Analyze the mystery chord against the Major 13th chord.
Step 4: Place the intervals in the correct numerical sequence that resembles the uneven number sequence of a chord

---

TUTORIAL

Let's use the mystery chord tones [E–A–D–F–B] as a tutorial example.
What is the name of this chord?

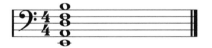

To analyze this chord completely, one must build up a 13th chord from each note and do an analysis against each 13th chord. As E is the lowest note, this should be our first starting point.

Analogy from E
Step 1
E being the root, we use the E Major scale as a reference.

Step 2
Build a Major 13th chord on the chosen E root, in this case E∆13.

13	C#
11	A
9	F#
7	D#
5	B
3	G#
1	E

Step 3
Analyze the mystery chord tones against the Major 13th chord.
Mystery chord tones [E – A – D – F – B]
Analogy   Root 11   ♭7   ♭9   5th

Step 4
Place the intervals in the correct numerical order. The A in the E Major scale is the 11, but as there is no 3rd the A must be a sus4. This gives us (1 – 4 – 5 – ♭7 – ♭9) and the chord is called E7sus♭9. Voiced : E – A – D – F – B
                          1   4   ♭7 ♭9 5

Confusingly, there are other options, even though this would be our first option, as the chord makes sense. If we took some of the other notes and treated them as the root — this is what happens:

Analogy from A
Step 1
If A were the root we would use the A Major scale as a reference.

            1   2(9)   3   4(11)   5   6(13)   7   8

Step 2
Build a Major 13th chord on the chosen A root, in this case A∆13.

13	F#
11	D
9	B
7	G#
5	E
3	C#
1	A

Step 3

Analyze the mystery chord tones against the Major 13th chord.

Mystery chord tones [E – A – D – F – B]

Analogy   5th   Root 11   **?**   9th

Step 4

Place the intervals in the correct numerical order. What then is F? Counting up the A major scale, F is the ♭6 (♭13). We would not call the ♭6 a #5 as we already have a 5th. As there is no 3rd, the D must be a sus4 so we have 1 – 4 – 5 – 9 add ♭13. This chord has no 7th or 6th to support the upper extensions and if we made the 4th the 11th there would be no 3rd. So this is an awkward chord compared to E7sus♭9 and would not be the obvious first choice chord name.

The rest of the notes, D, F and B

If we did the analogy using the same system starting on D, we would arrive at the chord Dm6/9.

E – A – D – F – B

9   5   1 ♭3 6(13)

However, with the 9th being at the bottom, we can call this chord Dm6/E, a slash chord. Using the same system and working out the chord from the F we arrive at FΔ7♭5 (add 13). Not straight-forward and simple, and not a good choice. If B were the root and using the same system we arrive at BØadd11.

B – D – F – A – E

1 ♭3 ♭5 ♭7 11

As E (the 11th) should be in the bass, this chord is better seen as a slash chord BØ/E.

Conclusion: With E being the lowest note, the E7sus♭9 is the best choice.

6.5
SEVENTH CHORDS BUILT ON THE MAJOR SCALE

On each degree of the major scale we can build a seventh chord. Here they are in the key of C from the bottom up:

Position	Chord tones	Symbol
VII	B – D – F – A	BØ
VI	A – C – E – G	Am7
V	G – B – D – F	G7
IV	F – A – C – E	FΔ7
III	E – G – B – D	Em7
II	D – F – A – C	Dm7
I	C – E – G – B	CΔ7

I   II   III   IV   V   VI   VII

6.6
THE II–V–I PROGRESSION

This chord progression, the most popular and most used in jazz, is also found in many other types of music. Before we look at the II–V–I progression, we have to first understand the V7–I cadence, known as the perfect cadence in classical music theory. This progression has a strong resolution from the 5th degree chord of the scale to the tonic chord (e.g. G dominant 7 to C).

THE PERFECT CADENCE

Question: Why does a perfect cadence (V7–I) have such a strong resolving feel?
Answer: In a major scale, the 7th note is called a leading note and wants to resolve to the upper tonic. Also the 4th note wants to resolve down to the 3rd. Notice that in both cases, the resolving note is only a semi-tone away.

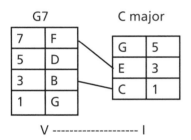

The perfect cadence has:
1) the leading note resolving to the tonic (B to C), and
2) the sus4 resolving to the 3rd (F to E).

THE II–V-I PROGRESSION

By placing the II chord (Dm) in front of this cadence we create the II–V–I progression.

Observations: The II chord is always minor.
The V chord is always a dominant7.
The II–V does not need to end with I.

In jazz the consecutive II–V–I progressions do not need to relate to one another's keys.

For example: We could have a II–V–I in the key of C followed by a II–V–I in the key of B♭.

Dm7 G7	CΔ7	Cm7 F7	B♭Δ7
II V	I	II V	I

THE II–V RE-HARMONIZATION

When a dominant chord fills up 2 or more beats, it can be reharmonised by adding its related II chord on half of the space before it. This re-harmonization can be done, for example, on the first six bars of the tune *Early Autumn*.

Original

CΔ7	B7	B♭Δ7	A7	A♭Δ7	G7

Re-harmonisation

CΔ7	F♯m7 B7	B♭Δ7	Em7 A7	A♭Δ7	Dm7 G7
	II ------- V		II ------ V		II ------- V

This re-harmonization can be applied to the V of V progression. See page 211.

THE SECONDARY DOMINANT

Good music composition and improvisation usually has a balance between tension and release. This can be created in many ways using for example, harmony (the orchestration and progressions), simple or complex rhythms, dynamics or specific tempi. Dissonance can be felt as a tension, and going to a consonance sound will be the release or resolution. As we see on page 195, a perfect cadence is a dominant chord leading to the tonic I chord. This gives us that tension and release forward motion feel even though the dominant chord is not really that dissonant.

Question: What is a secondary dominant?
Answer: A Secondary Dominant Chord is a dominant 7th chord that is a fifth away from a diatonic chord other than the tonic. For example, in the key of C the V–I perfect cadence would be G7 to the C major chord. A secondary dominant in the same key could be A7 to Dm7, (a diatonic chord other than the tonic).

Again, here are the diatonic seventh chords in the key of C major.

CΔ	Dm7	Em7	FΔ	G7	Am7	BØ	CΔ

Let's place a secondary dominant 7th chord before each diatonic chord, creating a series of V–Is.
Note: *A half-diminished chord does not sound good as a I chord so let's exclude the BØ, and place a dominant 7 chord before a dominant 7 to create a V of V, (D7 – G7) explained on page 211.*

CΔ	A7	Dm7	B7	Em7	C7	FΔ	D7	G7	E7	Am7	BØ	CΔ
	V ------ I		V ----- I		V ----- I		V ------- I		V ------- I			

What secondary dominants do is create a slight tension and release on to each diatonic chord.

SECONDARY DOMINANT SLASH CHORDS

Putting the 3rd of each secondary dominant chord into the bass turning it into a slash chord, creates a great chromatic bass line movement.

CΔ	A7/C#	Dm7	B7/D#	Em7	C7/E	FΔ	D7/F#	G7	E7/G#	Am7	BØ	CΔ

6.7
CYCLES

THE CYCLE OF FIFTHS IN CLASSICAL THEORY ...

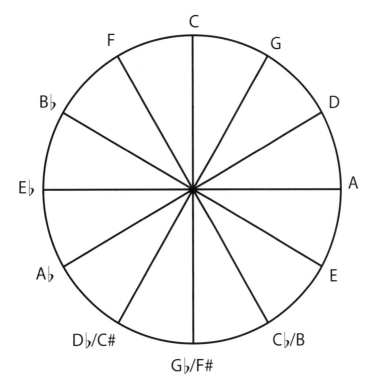

Starting on C major, going up a perfect 5th, we arrive at the note G. Make this G the tonic note of G major (the key with one sharp). From G go up another perfect 5th to D (two sharps). From D, go up another perfect 5th and get A (three sharps), and so on. In the same way, the key a 5th below C is F major and has one flat, and a 5th below F major is B♭ major with its two flats, and so on. This key signature clock is useful for learning key signatures.

... BECOMES THE CYCLE OF FOURTHS IN JAZZ (Simply refered to as the CYCLES)

Jazz musicians, however, use the cycle clock anti-clockwise, as the movement from note to note follows the roots of the II-V-I progression.
From C play up a 4th till F. From F play up a 4th to B♭. From B♭ play up a 4th till E♭ and so on. We count up but go backwards around the clock.
Practice your scales and arpeggios using the cycle of 4ths to memorise the sound as well as the cycle movement.

C - F - B♭ - E♭ - A♭ - D♭ - G♭ - B - E - A - D - G

II - V - I
    II - V - I
        II - V - I ...etc.

6.8
MODES DERIVED FROM THE MAJOR SCALE

If we play all the white notes on a piano from C to C, which is the major scale, we can work out a formula counting the number of tones and semitones going up from C to C. As in the major scale intervals, all modes are derived, named and matched according to the white notes (in the key of C) on the keyboard. If we play all the white notes starting on the 2nd position of C major, D up to D, we derive the 2nd mode. Do the same with the 3rd position, E to E (remember just white notes), then F to F, etc.
Each one of these positions has a modal name and it's own formula.

In the key of C (*T stands for tone, st stands for semi-tone*).

Position	Notes	Name	Formulae
VII	B – B	Locrian	st-T-T-st-T-T-T
VI	A – A	Aeolian	T-st-T-T-st-T-T
V	G – G	Mixolydian	T-T-st-T-T-st-T
IV	F – F	Lydian	T-T-T-st-T-T-st
III	E – E	Phrygian	st-T-T-T-st-T-T
II	D – D	Dorian	T-st-T-T-T-st-T
I	C – C	Ionian	T-T-st-T-T-T-st

The above seven modes must eventually be transposed and played in all twelve keys using the formulae.

To understand the modes and the chords that are derived from them, we have to write down each mode from the same starting note, (in this case C) using the modal formulae above. Once we have done this we can then analyse each mode against the major scale with the same root note, (in this case C major) to have an understanding of each scale.

ANALYSING A SCALE/MODE using the major scale as a reference.

    Step 1. Write down C major scale (the reference scale) with its interval numbers on top of each note.
    Step 2. Write down the mode using its formula starting on C.
    Step 3. Compare the two scales and write down the interval numbers with the changes under the mode you are analysing.
    Step 4. Circle the intervals 1 – 3 – 5 – 7 to see which seventh chord is derived from the mode. These notes are called CHORD TONES because they define the quality of each 7th chord.

Then further:
    Step 5. Analyse the upper extensions (those in-between notes).

Mode I
IONIAN – MAJOR SCALE

Before we analyze the other modes let's look at the major scale

C	D	E	F	G	A	B
1	2	3	4	5	6	7
	(9)		(11)		(13)	

The 7th chord derived from this mode is C∆7.
Because this chord comes from the first mode, it is called a I chord. The avoid note is the 4th, F.

Mode II
DORIAN

	1	2	3	4	5	6	7
Reference major scale:	C	D	E	F	G	A	B
DORIAN analyzed:	C	D	E♭	F	G	A	B♭
	1	2	♭3	4	5	6	♭7
		(9)		(11)		(13)	

The 7th chord derived from this mode is Cmin7.
Because this chord comes from the second mode, it is called a II chord.

Mode III
PHRYGIAN

	1	2	3	4	5	6	7
Reference major scale:	C	D	E	F	G	A	B
PHRYGIAN analyzed:	C	D♭	E♭	F	G	A♭	B♭
	1	♭2	♭3	4	5	♭6	♭7
		(♭9)		(11)		(♭13)	

The 7th chord derived from this mode is Cmin7.
Because this chord comes from the third mode, it is called a III chord.
This scale is a little deceiving. Go to page 205 to have an understanding of the Phrygian scale.

Mode IV
LYDIAN

	1	2	3	4	5	6	7
Reference major scale:	C	D	E	F	G	A	B
LYDIAN analysed:	C	D	E	F#	G	A	B
	1	2	3	#4	5	6	7
		(9)		(#11)		(13)	

The7th chords derived from this mode are C∆7♭5 or C∆#11.
Because this chord comes from the fourth mode, it is called a IV chord.

Mode V
MIXOLYDIAN

	1	2	3	4	5	6	7
Reference major scale:	C	D	E	F	G	A	B
MIXOLYDIAN analyzed:	C	D	E	F	G	A	B♭
	1	2	3	4	5	6	♭7
		(9)		(11)		(13)	

The 7th chord derived from this mode is C7.
Because this chord comes from the fifth mode, it is called a V chord. The avoid note is the 4th, F.

Mode VI
AEOLIAN (natural minor)

	1	2	3	4	5	6	7
Reference major scale:	C	D	E	F	G	A	B
AEOLIAN analyzed:	C	D	E♭	F	G	A♭	B♭
	1	2	♭3	4	♭5	♭6	♭7
		(9)		(11)		(♭13)	

The 7th chord derived from this mode is Cmin7.
Because this chord comes from the sixth mode, it is called a VI chord. Notice the ♭6. When we have a minor chord with a ♭6 we use Aeolian.

Mode VII
LOCRIAN

	1	2	3	4	5	6	7
Reference major scale:	C	D	E	F	G	A	B
LOCRIAN analyzed:	C	D♭	E♭	F	G♭	A♭	B♭
	1	♭2	♭3	4	♭5	♭6	♭7
		(♭9)		(11)		(♭13)	

The 7th chord derived from this mode is C half-diminished, also known as Cmin7♭5. Because this chord comes from the seventh mode, it is called a VII chord. Playing the Cmin7♭5 chord in the left hand and a D♭ note an octave up with the right, you will hear another ♭9 avoid note interval. Therefore the 2nd note of the scale is an "avoid note".

SUMMARY of modal chords on a major scale.

Position	Chord	Symbol
VII	half-diminished	m7♭5 or Ø
VI	minor 7	m7 or −7
V	dominant 7	7
IV	major 7	Maj7 or 7
III	minor7	m7 or −7
II	minor7	m7 or −7
I	major7	Maj7 or 7

6.9
THE MINOR II-V-I CHORD PROGRESSION

To understand this progression we must firstly once again look at the 7th chords conceived from the seven modes of the major scale, using the key of C major.

I	II	III	IV	V	VI	VII
CΔ7	Dm7	Em7	FΔ7	G7	Am7	BØ

If we make the tonic key centre the "relative minor"* (Am7), that changes the number order of the chords as Am would now become the I chord and the key centre.

III	IV	V	VI	VII	I	II
CΔ7	Dm7	Em7	FΔ7	G7	Am7	BØ

Let's put the I chord at the beginning so that the numbers go from left to right.

I	II	III	IV	V	VI	VII
Am7	BØ	CΔ7	Dm7	Em7	FΔ7	G7

We now see that the II chord is BØ and the V chord is Em7 in the key of A minor. Therefore, making a II–V–I in this key we would get;

BØ Em7	Am7
II V	I

As one of the strongest resolution to a I chord is Dominant 7 to I and not V minor to I, we have to modify the above II-V-I, changing the Em7 into a dominant 7 chord by raising the minor 3rd to a major 3rd.

E7 = (E – **G#** – B – D). The G sharp being the leading note to the A.

BØ E7	Am7
II V	I

* The Aeolian scale and chord is the "relative minor" key to the tonic major key as it shares the same key signature as the major. The major is said to be the "relative major" to the minor. E.g. C major and A minor are relatives.

THE PHRYGIAN #3

Going back to our major modal system we saw that Em7 was conceived from the Phrygian mode (in C major).

We have raised G to G# so let's look at what scale we have now;

If we play this scale from A we find that this is the A Harmonic minor scale, and playing the scale from the 5th position we arrive at the above scale. Therefore, on the V7 chord we can play the PHRYGIAN #3 and like before, on a Half-diminished chord we play LOCRIAN.

Question: Why is it called Phrygian #3?
Answer: Because we took the Phrygian scale and sharpened the 3rd note. Another name for this scale is the SPANISH SCALE.

When we analyse this scale and block 7th chord chord-tones we get;

E7♭9 or E7#5 can be derived from this scale. These two chord types have a strong resolution to the Im or ImΔ, and the Phrygian#3 scale sounds beautiful on this progression.

(As the V7 is now an altered dominant chord, there are more improvisation options which we will look at once we have done the Melodic minor modes).

Question: What do we play on the minor I chord?

Answer:
THE MINOR I and the DORIAN MODE

If we played the white notes on the keyboard from D to D we get the D Dorian mode. Let's look at the analysed scale again.

D Dorian =

Now let's analyze the D Aeolian (the natural minor)

D Aeolian =   D – E – F – G – A – B♭ – C – D
              1   2   ♭3   4   5   ♭6   ♭7   8
                   (9)   (11)   (♭13)

The difference in the two scales is the 13th. On the Dorian mode we have all the natural notes of the minor chord as well as the natural upper extensions. For this reason, jazz musicians prefer the Dorian sound over the Aeolian on a minor 7th chord. The Aeolian sounds right but the Dorian sounds hip. Listen to Miles Davis' solo on his tune "So What."

Shortcut Tip: If we play any Aeolian scale and raise the 6th, we have Dorian.
Conclusion: On the I chord of a minor II-V-I, we can use the Dorian mode.

MINOR/MAJOR7 CHORD and the HARMONIC or MELODIC MINOR SCALE

When a minor chord is used as a I chord it can also be played as a min6 or a minΔ7 chord.

In the key of Cmajor, the AmΔ chord =   A – C – E – G#
                                             1   ♭3 5   7

Both Harmonic minor and Melodic minor can be used on this chord as all the chord tones of the minΔ chord are found in these scales.

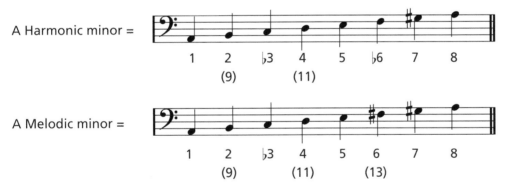

A Harmonic minor =
1   2   ♭3   4   5   ♭6   7   8
   (9)   (11)

A Melodic minor =
1   2   ♭3   4   5   6   7   8
   (9)   (11)   (13)

Notice the natural upper extensions of the melodic minor scale.

MINOR II–V–I SUMMARY

Position	Chord	Scale
IIØ	IIØ	LOCRIAN
V	V7♭9 or V7#5	PHRYGIAN #3 (for now)
I	min7 or min6 or minΔ7	DORIAN, HARMONIC or MELODIC MINOR

Note: The minor II-V. i.e. IIØ–V7♭9 can sometimes also lead to a I major7, as in the ending of "Stella by Starlight."

CØ / F7♭9 /	B♭Δ7	

6.10

THE DIMINISHED AND V7♭9 CHORD SUBSTITUTION

The V7♭9 chord can be, and is usually, the V chord of a minor II–V–I progression, for e.g. A7♭9 – Dm7, or A7♭9 – DmΔ7. However, let's take a closer look at the V7♭9 chord using A7♭9 for the analyses.

A7♭9 = A – C# – E – G – B♭

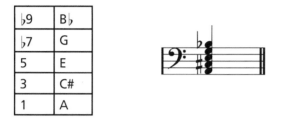

If we take away the root of this chord, the A note, we would be left with

This chord is a C# diminished 7.

Because of the four similar notes in the two chords, they are related and therefore, when we see a V7♭9 chord it can in some cases be substituted by its related diminished chord (or visa versa). The usual case can be found on a I–VI–II–V chord progression* as in the tune "Stormy Weather."

The chords on the 1st two bars of *Stormy Weather* are:

FΔ D7♭9	Gm7 C7

We can create chromatic movement by leaving out the root note (D) of the D7♭9 chord resulting in a F#dim7.

FΔ F#dim7	Gm7 C7

Improv note: The 'D Phrygian #3' scale, which works beautifully over the D7♭9 chord leading to the Gm7, sounds just as beautiful when played over the F#dim7.
Short cut tip: When you see a dim7 chord, go down a major 3rd from its root to get the V7♭9 substitution.

*See page 228

Another two examples can be found on the first five bars of the tune "How Insensitive."

Dm9	/ / / /	C#dim	/ / / /	Cm6	/ / / /
		(A7♭9)		Dorian	

The major 3rd down from C# is A. Therefore, we can play an A Phrygian #3 over the C#dim,

or

on the first three bars of the bridge of the tune "Softly as in a Morning Sunrise."

E♭maj7	/ / / /	Edim	/ / / /	Fm7	/ / / /
		(C7♭9)			

Question: How do we know when to use diminished scale or the Phyrgian #3?
Answer: Our ears and heart will tell us, and not the theory.

6.11
SUSPENDED 4TH

THE 7sus4 CHORD

When the 4th replaces the 3rd in a chord we call this a sus 4 chord: (1 – 4 – 5). Add the 7th and we have a 7sus4: (1 – 4 – 5 – ♭7). Unlike classical theory, where the 4th resolves to the 3rd, in Jazz and contemporary music the 4th does not need to resolve (see Herbie Hancock's tune "Maiden Voyage"). Because all the notes of a 7sus4 are found in the Mixolydian mode, we can use this mode on a 7sus4 chord.

C Mixolydian =

C7 sus =

Unlike a dominant 7 chord where the 4th note of the Mixolydian is an "avoid note", when played against a sus chord there is no avoid note. However, use your ears as the Mixolydian might be the wrong sound for a particular sus chord, "Maiden Voyage" is a good example.

Note: Musicians usually just write sus instead of sus4.

The 7sus4 CHORD that includes the 3rd

As we saw earlier, E to F an octave above is a ♭9 interval creating the avoid note. If we inverted this interval, in other words put the F on the bottom and the E an octave above we would simply have a major 7th interval and it now becomes possible to include the 3rd on a sus chord **if it is played above the 4th.**

For example: Csus with the 3rd on top.

3	E
b7	Bb
5	G
4	F
1	C

Major 7 interval

The 9sus SLASH CHORD

This chord is the same as a 7sus just with the 9th added (1 – 4 – 5 – ♭7 – 9). Because the 5th of this chord does not add anything to the character of the chord we can leave it out. Therefore, if we wrote out the notes of a C9sus chord leaving out the 5th we would have,

C – F – B♭ – D
1 – 4 – ♭7 – 9

This is a 2nd inversion B♭ major triad (B♭ – D – F) over a C bass note. In other words, play the root of the sus chord with your left hand and play the major triad a whole step below with your right hand.

$$F9\,sus\ =\ E\flat/F\ =\ \frac{\overset{\flat7\ -\ 9\ -\ 4}{E\flat\ -\ G\ -\ B\flat}}{F}$$
(root)

and we can improvize on the F Mixolydian mode.

The Sus ♭9 CHORD AND THE PHRYGIAN MODE (Mode III)

When analysing the Phrygian mode we found the 7th chord to be a minor 7th. However, this mode is not used over a minor chord, but rather a sus♭9 chord.

Let's look at the E Phrygian mode and the Esus♭9 chord.

E Phrygian =

Esus♭9 =

E	F	A	B	D
1	♭9	4	5	♭7

THE SUS♭9 as a V, to the I CHORD, PROGRESSION

Sus ♭9 chords can also be played as a V chord leading to I or Im△.

For example: Gsus♭9 to C△7

Gsus♭9 to Cm△7

Shortcut tip: Play the Aeolian scale and lower the 2nd note to get the Phrygian scale.

6.12
TRITONE

If we halve the octave, i.e. the middle note between C and C octave, we get the note F sharp. The interval from C to F sharp is called an augmented 4th. Another name for this interval is THE TRITONE INTERVAL. An easy way to find the tritone note is to play a major scale up from the tonic to the 4th note and sharpen it, or as the name implies, go up three tones.

From the tonic note of E the tritone would be an A sharp (enharmonic B flat). Notice that this interval is found in the C7, a dominant chord, between the 3rd and the ♭7th.
Because the tritone is exactly half the octave if you invert the interval, i.e. put the 3rd above the ♭7, it would still be a tritone interval (an augmented 4th). What makes these two notes interesting is that they belong to two different dominant chords.

THE TRITONE DOMINANT CHORDS.

If we were to construct a dominant chord on the tritone interval of a dominant chord, this new chord would be a tritone chord and these two chords would be related.

Question: Why are they related?
Answer: Let's analyze each chord to get the answer using C7 and a chord built on its tritone, the F#7.

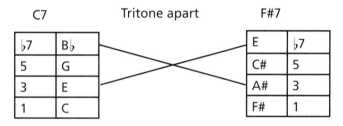

We can see that the two most important notes of a seventh chord, the 3rd and the b7, are found in both chords.
- The 3rd of C7 (E) is the same as the ♭7 (E) of F#7.
- The ♭7 of C7 (B♭) is the same enharmonic note as the 3rd (A#) of F#7.

On dominant chords it is common to alter the 5th or the 9th, so let's add a ♭9 to each tritone chord making them dominant7♭9 chords.

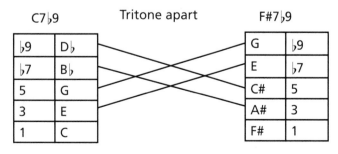

- The 3rd of C7 (E) is the same as the ♭7 (E) of F#7.
- The 5th of C7 (G) is the same as the ♭9 (G) of F#7.
- The ♭7 of C7 (B♭) is the same enharmonic note as the 3rd (A#) of F#7.
- The ♭9 (D♭) is the same enharmonic note as the 5th (C#) of F#7.

The only difference between these two chords, is the roots.

Now let's analyse a dominant7♭5 tritone.

C7♭9   Tritone apart   F#7♭5

♭7	B♭		E	♭7
♭5	G♭		C	♭5
3	E		A#	3
1	C		F#	1

The related notes are now:
- The Root of C7 (C) is the same note as the ♭5 (C) of F#7.
- The 3rd of C7 (E) is the same as the ♭7 (E) of F#7.
- The ♭5 of C7 (G♭) is the same enharmonic note as the root (F#) of F#7.
- The ♭7 of C7 (B♭) is the same enharmonic note as the 3rd (A#) of F#7.

As all four notes of each chord are duplicated these two chords are actually identical.

Question: Why do we use tritones?
Answer: Re-harmonising a chord sequence with tritones can make the melody line more interesting. For example, where the melody note is the 5th on a dominant chord (an uninteresting note), if we reharmonise the chord with the tritone, then the melody note becomes a ♭9, which has a more interesting sound.

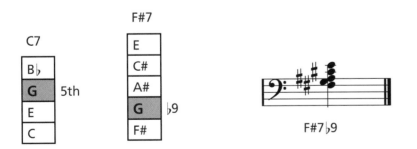

We also use tritones if we want to create a chromatic bass line on a II–V progression.
For example on the first four bars of the tune "One Note Samba."

Dm7 D♭7	Cm7 B7

is actually just:

Dm7 G7	Cm7 F7
II V	II V

The D♭7 is a tritone substitution of G7.
The B7 is a tritone substitution of F7.

Here is another example of the turnaround on the Miles Davis version of "Someday My Prince Will Come."

Original:

Cm7 F7	B♭Δ7
II V	I

Changed:

Cm7 B7	B♭Δ7
II Tritone	I
of V	

Another example can be found on the bridge of the tune "Autumn Leaves."

6.13
V of V

So far we have learnt the sound of a V–I or II–V–I progression where the dominant V chord leads to the I that is either a major or minor 7th chord. There is another popular progression called the V of V, where the dominant V chord leads to the I that is also a dominant 7th chord type. For example, G7 to C7.

This progression can be seen as moving down a 5th, however, most V of V progressions follow the cycle of 4ths, so it is best to see the chords moving up a 4th around the cycle, i.e. G7 – C7 – F7 – B♭7 – E♭7, etc. The most popular use of V of V around the cycle can be found on the bridge of George Gershwin's composition, "I've Got Rhythm."

D7	/ / / /	G7	/ / / /	C7	/ / / /	F7	/ / / /

Sometimes musicians re-harmonise this progression using II – Vs.

Am7	D7	Dm7	G7	Gm7	C7	Cm7	F7
II------------V		II------------V		II------------V		II------------V	

V of V TRITONE HARMONY

Because these chords are all dominant 7ths, they each have a tritone-related chord. Using tritones on V of V creates voice-leading harmony.

D7	/ / / /	G7	/ / / /	C7	/ / / /	F7	/ / / /

Re-harmonisation

D7	A♭7	G7	D♭7	C7	G♭7	F7	B7
	tritone of D7		tritone of G7		tritone of C7		tritone of F7

Remember that dominant tritones can have altered notes, therefore going around the cycles using dominant 7♭5 chords sound great.

D7♭5	A♭7(♭5)	G7♭5	D♭7(♭5)	C7♭5	G♭7(♭5)	F7♭5	B7♭5

6.14
THE SYMMETRICAL SCALES

THE CHROMATIC SCALE

This scale is a twelve-note scale with the SYMMETRICAL formula (semi-tone / semi-tone) repeated. This scale is usually used together with other scales to create more mature and interesting music.

THE WHOLE-TONE SCALE

This scale is a six-note scale with the SYMMETRICAL formula (tone / tone) repeated. Let's analyse the scale starting on C.

	1	2	3	4	5	6	7
Ref. scale – Major:	C	D	E	F	G	A	B
Whole-tone scale:	C	D	E	F#	G#		B♭
	1	2	3	#4	#5		♭7

We see that the chord tones of C7#5 (1 – 3 – #5 – ♭7) are found in the scale. We therefore can use this scale over Augmented and Dominant Augmented chords. (i.e. C+, C7+5). Because this is a symmetrical scale, starting a whole-tone scale from each of the six notes, would, in fact produce the same scale. The same would happen when building the scale a semi-tone up. Therefore, there are in practice only two whole-tone scales.

The augmented dominant chord can be used as the V chord on a minor V–I.
For example: G7+5 to CmΔ7.

THE DIMINISHED SCALE

This scale is an eight-note scale with the SYMMETRICAL formula (tone / semi-tone) repeated. Because this scale has eight notes, an alphabet note (besides the root) has to be repeated. Let's analyse the scale starting on C.

	1	2	3	4	5		6	7
Ref. scale - Major:	C	D	E	F	G		A	B
Diminished scale:	C	D	E♭	F	G♭	A♭	A	B
	1	2	♭3	4	♭5	♭6	6	7
						(♭♭7)		

We see that the chord tones of Cdim7 (1 – ♭3 – ♭5 – ♭♭7) are found in the scale. We therefore can use this scale over Diminished and Diminished 7th chords. (i.e. Cdim, C°7). The symmetric principle of diminished harmony found on **page 185** also applies to this scale, i.e., C, E♭, G♭ and A diminished scales would all have the same notes, and in practice there are only three diminished scales.

THE DIMINISHED BLUES SCALE

Also known as the **HALF-STEP / WHOLE-STEP DIMINISHED** or the
8 NOTE DOMINANT SCALE

This scale is an eight-note scale with the SYMMETRICAL formula (semi-tone / tone) repeated. Because this scale has eight notes, an alphabet note (besides the root) has to be repeated when we write out the scale. Let's analyse the scale starting on C.

	1	2		3	4		5	6	7
Ref. scale – Major:	C	D		E	F		G	A	B
Dim. Blues scale:	C	D♭	D#	E	F#		G	A	B♭
	1	♭9	#9	3	#4(#11)		5	6	♭7

The 7th chord derived from this mode is C7. However this scale also has a ♭9, #9, ♭5. This scale therefore goes with a dominant 7th chord that has a ♭9, #9 or #11, which is usually only written as 7♭9. Important to note that there is no #5.

The diminished blues scale can be played on the V chord of a II-V-I progression.

6.15
THE PENTATONIC SCALE

The Pentatonic scale consists of five notes only. There are many different pentatonic scales, but the two most used in Western music are found within the major scale.

MAJOR PENTATONIC

If we take the 4th and 7th notes out of the major scale we have the Major Pentatonic scale.

C Major Pentatonic = C – D – E – G - A
                      1   2   3   5   6
                         (9)

If we were to play every single note at the same time we would have a 6/9 major chord, so this is the obvious chord that this scale is played on. However, this scale can also be played on a 7th, and because the scale has no 7th, this scale can be played on either a Major 7th or a dominant 7th chord.

MINOR PENTATONIC

The Minor Pentatonic scale has the same notes but starts on the 6th degree of the Major Pentatonic, (like the relative minor is related to the relative major). Making the A the tonic note of A Minor Pentatonic we arrive at the intervals:

A – C – D – E – G
1   ♭3   4   5   ♭7
       (11)

If we were to play every single note at the same time we would have a minor 7 add 11 chord, so a minor 7th is the obvious chord that this scale is played on. However, this scale can also be played on a 7sus, which gives it a bluesy sound. This scale sound is very close to the blues scale.

Question: What makes this scale different in character to the other scales?
Answer: Besides the whole-tone scale, this scale has no semi-tones, therefore it has no chromaticism and bigger intervallic jumps resulting in a feel of more space.

ADVANCED OPTIONS of the MAJOR & MINOR PENTATONIC SCALE

By playing the major or minor pentatonic on different degrees of various scales other than the root of that particular pentatonic, we are able to play the more interesting tensions in harmony. Here are two examples using the C major and A minor pentatonic.

THE MAJOR PENTATONIC PLAYED ON THE TRITONE

On a Dominant 7 alt chord, go up a tritone from the root and play a major pentatonic scale.
Example: C major pentatonic over G♭7 Alt chord

And here the interval analogy of C major pentatonic in relation to the G♭7alt chord.

```
  G♭7alt = G♭ – B♭ – (C or D) – E – (G or A)
            1    3     ♭5   #5   ♭7   ♭9   #9
C major pentatonic = C  –  D  –  E  –  G  –  A
                     ♭5    #5    ♭7    ♭9    #9
```

THE MINOR PENTATONIC PLAYED ON THE MAJOR 7TH DEGREE.

On a Major 13 #11 chord, play a minor pentatonic down a semitone from the chords root.
Example: A minor pentatonic played over B♭Δ13(#11).

```
B♭ Maj 13(#11) =  B♭ – D – F – A – C – E – G
                   1    3   5   7   9  #11 13
```

And here the interval analogy of A minor pentatonic in relation to the B♭Δ13 (#11) chord.

```
A minor pentatonic = A – C – D – E – G
                     7   9   3  #11 13
```

IMPROV IDEA:

Experiment playing the A minor pentatonic over this chord progression:

B♭Δ13#11	BØ E7♭9

6.16
THE BLUES

Question: Why is the Blues an important art form?
Answer: The Blues was one of the main influences in the birth of Jazz.

Question: What is the Blues?
Answer: The Blues mostly consists of a certain 12-bar progression played with a swing feel (triplets). The strange thing about the 12-bar Blues is that all the chords including the I chord are dominant 7th chords and the scale that is usually played over a blues has, in theory, very little in common with a dominant chord.

Let's first look at the progression and then the scale. The progression usually consists of three sets of four bars each, using chords from the I, IV and V degrees of the scale.
Set one: consists of four bars of I7.
Set two: consists of two bars of IV7 and two bars of I7.
Set three: consists of one bar of V7, then one bar of IV7, then two bars of I7.

However:
Blues players sometimes add a IV7 chord in bar 2, this is called the "**Quick Change.**" If we put a V7 chord in the last bar then that will result in a V–I when going back to the top; we call this a "**Turnaround.**"

THE 12 BAR BLUES PROGRESSION
(Note: all chords are dominant 7th.)

* Quick change

I	IV	I	𝄎
IV	𝄎	I	𝄎
V	IV	I	(V)

* Turnaround

Example in the key of C

C7	F7	C7	𝄎
F7	𝄎	C7	𝄎
G7	F7	C7	G7

The Jazz Blues evolved out of this blues as well as other styles such as "Soul" and "Rock and Roll." This chord progression has to be internalized.

12 BAR BEBOP JAZZ BLUES progression:

The Jazz Blues is simply an embellishment of the 12-bar blues. To convert a 12-bar blues to a Jazz Blues follow these steps:

FORM AND ANALYSIS
Let's start with the 12-bar blues in the key of C (shown on previous page).
Step 1: Shift the V chord (G7) in bar 9 to bar 10 and add its related II chord on bar 9 creating a II-V, Dm7-G7.

C7	F7	C7	𝄎
F7	𝄎	C7	𝄎
Dm7	G7	C7	G7

  II   V

Step 2: On bar 4 (C7), do a II-V reharmonisation, i.e. Gm7-C7 that leads to F7, V7 of V7.

                                                    II   V

C7	F7	C7	Gm7 C7
F7	𝄎	C7	𝄎
Dm7	G7	C7	G7

Step 3: Treat the Dm7 chord in bar 9 as a minor I chord and place a minor II-V in front of it in bar 8, i.e. Em7♭5-A7-Dm7.

C7	F7	C7	Gm7 C7
F7	𝄎	C7	Em7♭5 A7
			II V
Dm7	G7	C7	G7

Step 4: Add a III-VI-II-V turnaround of the tonic key in the last 2 bars.

C7	F7	C7	Gm7 C7
F7	𝄎	C7	Em7♭5 A7
Dm7	G7	Em7 A7	Dm7 G7
		III VI	II V

Step 5: Lastly, add a #IV degree dim7 in bar 6. *Notice the blues note is a #4 and also not all bebop blues changes have this #IVdim7 chord – some stay on the IV.*

C7	F7	C7	Gm7 C7
F7	F#dim7	C7	Em7♭5 A7
Dm7	G7	Em7 A7	Dm7 G7

Even though there are a lot more chords, the original 12-bar blues form can still be felt throughout.
Memorize it in all 12 keys, however, pay special attention to the horn player's favorites:
F, B♭, E♭ and C.

THE DESCENDING BLUES.
Also known as BIRD BLUES

This progression evolved out of the tune written by Charlie Parker called "Blues for Alice."
Unlike the first dominant chord of the 12-bar blues, this blues starts with a major 7 chord.
Notice the II-V's.

F△	EØ A7+9	Dm 7 D♭7	Cm 7 F 7
B♭7	B♭m7 E♭7	Am 7 D 7	A♭m7 D♭7
Gm 7	C 7	F 7 D 7	Gm 7 C 7

THE BLUES SCALE

The most common and oldest scale played on the blues is the Blues Scale.

    1   ♭3   4   #4   5   ♭7

We see that this scale consists of a minor 7th chord. However, it is not restricted to a minor 7th
and can virtually be played on almost anything, but mostly used on dominant 7th chords.
You can also play the blues scale a minor 3rd down from the root of any chord that a major
pentatonic scale can be played on, sort of like a relative minor.

Question: How can this scale be used on a Dominant 7 chord that has a major 3rd because the
blues scale has a minor 3rd?
Answer: That question cannot be explained. It is a secret of dissonance that we have to accept
in music. The Blues Scale is a scale about a certain vibe.

Question: What note makes this scale sound bluesy?
Answer: Besides the minor 3rd played against a major 3rd, it is the #4 that creates the blues
sound.

Playing the blues scale over the 12-bar blues results in another mystery. Not only does the Blues
Scale built on the I chord have little in common with that chord, but the same Blues Scale can be
played over the entire 12-bar blues. i.e. In the key of C, the three chords of a C blues are
chord I = C7, chord IV = F7, and chord V = G7. The C Blues Scale can be played over all three of
these chords.

Shortcut tip: The Blues Scale is a minor 7th chord with a 4th and a chromatic note between the
4th and the 5th.

THE MINOR BLUES

The Minor Blues also consists of 12 bars like the normal dominant 12-bar blues progression. However, as the title explains, it has a minor sound.

Question: What gives this blues a minor sound?
Answer: The I chord of the first 4 bars and the IV chord in bar 5 and 6 are minor 7ths, as well as the I chord in bars 7 & 8 and 11 & 12.

Im7	/ / / /	/ / / /	/ / / /
IVm7	/ / / /	Im7	/ / / /
		Im7	

THE DOMINANT 7 ON A MINOR BLUES

If the V chord were a minor7, it would not have the strong gravity pull towards the I chord that a normal dominant 7 chord leading to a I chord produces. Therefore, for this reason, the V chord in a minor 12-bar blues remains a normal dominant 7. However, in a normal blues the V dominant 7 appears in bar 9 but in a minor blues it is delayed by a bar, being played in bar 10. The turnaround stays the same, i.e.: V7 on bar 12.

Question: Which chord is played in bar 9?
Answer: A V7 chord a semitone up, i.e. the flattened VI7 chord.

THE Minor 12-BAR BLUES PROGRESSION

Im7	/ / / /	/ / / /	/ / / /
IVm7	/ / / /	Im7	/ / / /
♭VI7	V7	Im7	V7

Example in the key of Cm

Cm7	/ / / /	/ / / /	/ / / /
Fm7	/ / / /	Cm7	/ / / /
A♭7	G7	Cm7	G7

We have already seen, when studying the minor II–V–I progression, that a 7♭9 chord has a strong gravity pull onto a tonic minor 7 chord. For this reason it is possible to put a 7♭9 chord one bar before each tonic minor 7th.

Example in the key of Cm

Cm7	/ / / /	/ / /	C7♭9
Fm7	/ / / /	Cm7	/ / / /
A♭7	G7	Cm7	G7♭9

An example of the above progression can be found in the tunes "Equinox" and "Mr P.C." by John Coltrane, two pieces that are nearly always played at jam sessions.
Note: The original version of "Equinox" is in the key of C#minor, however, at jam sessions it is played in the key of C minor.

VARIATIONS

1)   Tritones: sometimes the dominant chords in bar 9 and 10 can be substituted with the tritone harmony.
      For example in the key of Cm, bar 9 & 10 would be

D7	D♭7

2)   Another variation would be to play a ♭III7 & VI7♭5 in bar 9 and then play the ♭VI7 & V7 in bar 10.
      For example in the key of Cm:

E♭7 A7♭5	A♭7 G7

      An example of this can be found in the tune "Carrot Cake" by Peter Bernstein.

3)   The IVm7 chord in bar 5 & 6 can also be played as a sus7.

THE BLUES WALTZ

The word "Waltz" describes the feel i.e. 3/4.
The word "Blues" describes the form i.e. 12 bar blues.

A Blues Waltz is actually 24 bars long, but to maintain the blues form (which consists of 12 bars) we have to join every second 3/4 bar together creating bars of 6/4, the feel being two pulses per bar. Like this there will be 12 bars and we now have the normal dominant 12-bar blues progression. Therefore the pulse is 6/4 but the feel is still 3/4 swing.
The 3/4 feel can further be halved, i.e. a dotted quarter plus a dotted quarter to create a 4 against 6 feel (or a 2 against 3).

6/4 pulse =

| 1 | + | 2 | + | 3 | + | 4 | + | 5 | + | 6 | + |

4 against 6 feel =
(Swing feel)

| 1 | + | 2 | + | 3 | + | 4 | + | 5 | + | 6 | + |

Another feel: shift the notes by an eight note

THE MINOR BLUES WALTZ (6/4)

The Minor Blues Waltz has the same chord progression as the 12 bar minor blues.

6/4	Im7	/ / / /	/ / / /	/ / / /
	IVm7	/ / / /	Im7	/ / / /
	bVI7	V7	Im7	/ / / /

Note: One can also add tritone substitutions in bar 9 & 10.

An example in the key of Cm.

6/4	Cm7	/ / / /	/ / / /	/ / / /
	Fm7	/ / / /	Cm7	/ / / /
	Ab7	G7	Cm7	/ / / /

Tritones = D7   Db7

A good example of this is the minor blues by Wayne Shorter titled "Footprints." (This is how most musicians play it but actually the original has a lot more chords in the last four bars.)

THE IMPROV:- A good place to start would be C Dorian on Cm7, F Dorian on Fm7, and Mixolydian on the dominant chords. Also the C blues can be played over all the chords.

THE DOMINANT 7 BLUES WALTZ (6/4)

The Dominant Blues Waltz is very similar to the minor 6/4 but uses dominant7 chords.

6/4	C7	/ / / /	/ / / /	/ / / /
	F7	/ / / /	C7	/ / / /
	Ab7	G7	G7	/ / / /
	bVI7	V7		

A good example is the Miles Davis tune, *All Blues*. Notice the use of the bVI 7#9 and V7#9.

6/4	G7	/ / / /	/ / / /	/ / / /
	C7	/ / / /	G7	/ / / /
	D7(#9)	Eb7(#9) D7(#9)	G7	/ / / /

IMPROV NOTES: Mixolydian can be played on each dominant as well as the G blues and the blues starting a minor 3rd down, i.e. E blues. On the (7#9) chords, you can use whole tone and altered scales. "Footprints" and "All Blues" are jam session favorites, memorize these tunes.

6.17
THE JAZZ MELODIC MINOR SCALE
and the modes generated by it

In Western classical theory the Melodic Minor scale is a natural minor scale that when ascending, raises the 6th and 7th notes and lowers them on the way down. However, in Jazz Theory the Melodic Minor scale has a raised 6th and 7th going up as well as down. (In Jazz Theory the minor with the lowered 6th and 7th is called the Aeolian scale or natural minor.)

The Melodic Minor scale is a seven-note scale with seven modes that have greater melodic and intervallic possibilities than the major scale even though the only difference between the Melodic Minor and the major scale is that the Melodic Minor has a minor 3rd.

Shortcut tip — A shortcut to the Melodic Minor is to play a major scale and lower the 3rd to a minor 3rd.

If we were to play up the scale starting on the 2nd position of C melodic minor, D up till D, we derive the 2nd melodic minor mode. Do the same with the 3rd position of C melodic minor, E♭ to E♭, then F to F, etc. Each one of these positions has a modal melodic minor name and it's own formula.

Here are the formulas of each mode using C melodic minor.

Position	Note	Formula
VII	B – B	st - T - st - T - T - T - T
VI	A – A	T - st - T - st - T - T - T
V	G – G	T - T - st - T - st - T - T
IV	F – F	T - T - T - st - T - st - T
III	E♭ – E♭	T - T - T - T - st - T - st
II	D – D	st - T - T - T - T - st - T
I	C – C	T - st - T - T - T - T - st

The above seven modes must eventually be transposed and played in all twelve keys using the formulae.

To understand the modes and the chords that are derived from them, we have to write down each mode from the same starting note (in this case C) using the modal formulas above. Once we have done this we can then analyse each mode against the major scale with the same root note, (in this case C major) to have an understanding of each scale.

ANALYZING THE SEVEN MELODIC MINOR MODES:

Using the major scale as a reference.

Mode I – The MELODIC MINOR

	1	2	3	4	5	6	7
Reference major scale	C	D	E	F	G	A	B
MELODIC MINOR	C	D	E♭	F	G	A	B
	1	2	♭3	4	5	6	7
		(9)		(11)		(13)	

The 7th chord derived from this mode is **Cmin/Maj7.** (C-Δ, CmΔ7.) You can play this scale over this chord. Notice the natural upper extensions.

Mode II – The DORIAN ♭9

	1	2	3	4	5	6	7
Reference major scale	C	D	E	F	G	A	B
DORIAN ♭9	C	D♭	E♭	F	G	A	B♭
	1	♭2	♭3	4	5	6	♭7

The 7th chord derived from this mode is Cm7. However, the sound of the scale dictates a **C7sus♭9** chord.
Even though the Phrygian scale is usually the preferred scale to use over this chord, this
Dorian ♭9 melodic minor mode also has a place in the improviser's and composer's sound pallet.

Mode III – The LYDIAN AUGMENTED

	1	2	3	4	5	6	7
Reference major scale	C	D	E	F	G	A	B
LYDIAN AUGMENTED	C	D	E	F#	G#	A	B
	1	2	3	#4	5#	6	7
				(#11)			

The 7th chord derived from this mode is **CMaj7#5.**
This chord is sometimes notated as a slash chord, i.e. a triad over a bass note.
For example:
CMaj7#5 = C – E – G# – B   is the same as $\frac{E - G\# - B}{C}$ = E/C

Also CMaj9#5 is the same as E7/C.

Notice that the scale has a #11, which is not found in the chord. The name of this mode is
descriptive of the scale sound, i.e. Lydian (♭5 or #11), and Augmented (#5) chord tone.

Mode IV – The LYDIAN DOMINANT

	1	2	3	4	5	6	7
Reference major scale	C	D	E	F	G	A	B
LYDIAN DOMINANT	C	D	E	F#	G	A	B♭
	[1]	2	[3]	#4	[5]	6	[♭7]
				(#11)			

The 7th chord derived from this mode is C7, however, this scale also has a Lydian sound because it has a #4 (#11), therefore on a Dominant chord with a #11 (**C7#11**) we play the Lydian Dominant scale. The name of this mode is descriptive of the scale sound i.e. Lydian (♭5 or #11), and the Dominant (♭7) chord tone.

TRITONE. This chord has the same notes as the tritone chord that is built on mode VII, the Altered scale.

Mode V – The MIXOLYDIAN ♭13

(uncommonly used)

	1	2	3	4	5	6	7
Reference major scale	C	D	E	F	G	A	B
MIXOLYDIAN ♭13	C	D	E	F	G	A♭	B♭
	[1]	2	[3]	4	[5]	♭6	[♭7]
						(♭13)	

The 7th chord derived from this mode is C7, however the scale has a ♭6, which can be seen as a ♭13. Therefore, the 7th chord derived will be **C11♭13**. We can also treat the ♭6 as a #5 in the harmony of the chord (which is preferable) resulting in a **C7#5**, and the scale would fit nicely with this chord. This is not a popular scale among musicians, but try it.

Mode VI – LOCRIAN #2

	1	2	3	4	5	6	7
Reference major scale	C	D	E	F	G	A	B
LOCRIAN #2	C	D	E♭	F	G♭	A♭	B♭
	[1]	2	[♭3]	4	[♭5]	♭6	[♭7]
		(9)		(11)			

The 7th chord derived from this mode is **C Half-Diminished (CØ, Cm7♭5)**.
The difference between the half-diminished chord from the major scale modes and this one is that this scale has a NATURAL 9th, and therefore does not have an "avoid note". The actual chord is written as CØ9, or Cmin9♭5.

Mode VII – The ALTERED SCALE

Also known as the **SUPER LOCRIAN SCALE.**
Also known as the **DIMINISHED/WHOLE-TONE** scale because it starts out like a diminished scale and ends up like a whole-tone scale.

Diminished

st –T – st – T – T – T – T

Whole-tone

	1	2	3	4	5	6	7
Reference major scale	C	D	E	F	G	A	B♭
ALTERED SCALE	C	D♭	D#	E	F#	G#	B♭
	1	(♭9)	(#9)	3	#4	#5	♭7
					(♭5)		

The 7th chord derived from this mode is **C7#5.** However, this scale also has the other altered notes, ♭5, #9, ♭9. This scale therefore goes with a dominant 7th (♭5,#5,♭9,#9) chord, also known as an altered dominant chord, written **C7 Alt.**

TRITONE. This chord has the same notes as the tritone chord that is built on mode IV, the Lydian Dominant scale.

SUMMARY: in the key of C melodic minor.

Position	Chord	Scale
VII	B7alt	B Altered
VI	Aø9	A Locrian #2
V	C-Δ/ G bass	G Mixolydian ♭13
IV	F7#11	F Lydian Dominant
III	E♭Δ7#5	E♭ Lydian Augmented
II	D7sus♭9	D Dorian ♭9
I	C-Δ	C Melodic minor

THE NON-EXISTENT "AVOID NOTES" IN MELODIC MINOR HARMONY

In Melodic minor harmony the Major 3rd is lowered to a minor 3rd and the ♭9 is raised to the natural 9th on the Locrian#2. Because of this, there are no "avoid notes" in the Melodic minor modal system.

6.18
THE LYDIAN DOMINANT TRITONE IMPROVISATION

One can improvise on tritone harmony using the Lydian Dominant scale.

For example:
On the C7 the tritone is F#7 so we can therefore can use F# Lydian Dominant.

F# Lydian Dominant =

Lets analyse the F#Lydian Dominant against the C7 chord and relate the intervals to the C7 chord.

```
              1    3    5    ♭7
C7 Chord  = C – E –  G – B♭
```

F# Lydian Dominant = F# – G# – A# – B# – C# – D# – E – (F#)
In relation to C7   = ♭5   #5   ♭7   1   ♭9   #9   3

Because all the 5ths and 9ths are altered, this is a good choice scale for a C7alt chord.

Note: The F# Lydian Dominant scale is the tritone scale of the C Altered scale in the Melodic minor modal system.

6.19
BEBOP SCALES

If the chord tones (1 – 3 – 5 – 7) of a scale fall on the weak beats, (the "and"), it is musically better to add a note to the scale to shift them on to the stronger beats.

For example, if we play using 8th notes, a descending G Mixolydian scale, the ♭7 and other chord tones fall on the 'and'.

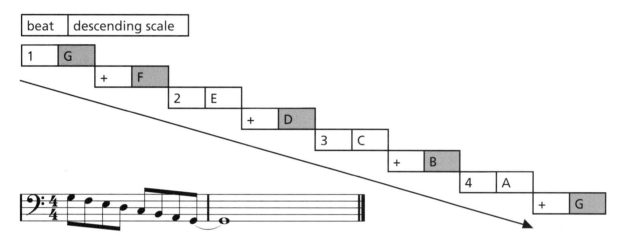

If we add an extra chromatic note before we play the ♭7, then the ♭7 falls on a downbeat making the phrase rhythmically smoother. Also, notice that the tonic note will then land on the first beat of the next bar.

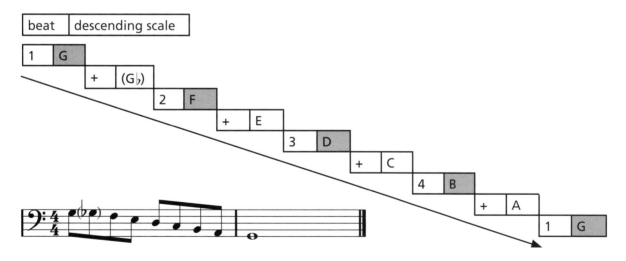

These scales with the extra chromatic note (making them 8 note scales) are called BEBOP SCALES. The most used bebop scales are the Bebop Major, Bebop Dorian and the Bebop Mixolydian. You can, however, add chromatic passing notes to any scale.

6.20
THE III–VI–II–V TURNAROUND

This turnaround consists of a set of chords that usually appears at the end of a piece of music, whether ending or returning to the top. These chords can also be used as a normal chord progression found within a tune. (The Roman numerals represent the position of the 7th chord, for example, in the key of C, the V means G7, etc).

The turnaround or III–VI–II–V chord progression is:

C7	A7	Dm7	G7	Em7♭5	A7♭9	Dm7	G7

Question: How did this progression evolve as it is not diatonic?
Answer: Let's look at the evolution in the key of C major.

The diatonic progression:

I	VI	II	V
Cmaj7	Am7	Dm7	G7

Because a dominant chord has more interesting altered possibilities for improvisation than a minor7, jazz musicians change the second chord into a dominant chord:

Cmaj7	A7	Dm7	G7

They then treat this A7 as a V chord in a II–V progression. This changes the Cmaj7 into Em7, the II chord in the progression, i.e.

II	V
Em7	A7

If we place the new chord progression after the first one we have:

C7	A7	Dm7	G7	Em7	A7	Dm7	G7

Because Em7 is the 3rd chord of the major diatonic chords, this progression became known as the III–VI–II–V progression.

If we play the chords Em7 – A7 – Dm7, then this is actually a minor II–V–I progression. Just as in a minor II–V–I progression where the II chord is half-diminished and the V chord V7♭9 or #5, the same would apply here.

Finally:

C7	A7	Dm7	G7	Em7♭5	A7♭9	Dm7	G7
I	VI	II	V	III	VI	II	V

Another option.
You can change a II chord that forms part of a II–V7 progression into a V chord on consecutive II–V's, creating V7 of V7. In other words, the V7 leading to a I chord that is also a dominant 7 chord.
i.e.

C7	A7	D7	G7	E7	A7	D7	G7

6.21
RHYTHM CHANGES

HISTORY

Around 1930, George Gershwin (the composer of another famous tune called "Summertime") composed a piece of music called "I've Got Rhythm" for the Broadway musical, "Girl Crazy." Jazz musicians discovered that it was fun to play over these chord changes and practically hijacked this piece of music, composing many different heads (melodies) over the changes, as well as embellishing the harmony slightly.

The tune consists of:
Two A sections built around the I–VI–II–V, III–VI–II–V progression,
a middle B section using the chord progression V of V starting a major 3rd up from the tonic key,
and then returning to an A section. Form = AABA
Here are the chords for "I've Got Rhythm."

A

B♭	G7	Cm7	F7	Dm7	G7	Cm7	F7
Fm7	B♭7	E♭△	E♭m	Dm7	G7	Cm7	F7

A

B♭	G7	Cm7	F7	Dm7	G7	Cm7	F7
Fm7	B♭7	E♭△	E♭m	Cm7	F7	B♭△	

B

D7		≿		G7		≿	
C7		≿		F7		≿	

A

B♭	G7	Cm7	F7	Dm7	G7	Cm7	F7
Fm7	B♭7	E♭△	E♭m	Cm7	F7	B♭	

Over the years the changes to this tune have been modified. However, it has never lost the sound and structure. Here is one of the variations on the A section:

A

B♭	B°7	Cm7	C#°7	Dm7	G7	Cm7	F7
B♭	B♭7/D	E♭	E°7	B♭/F	G7	Cm	F7

Listening: Dizzy Gillespie and Charlie Parker's, "Salt Peanuts."
Sonny Rollins's, "Oleo." (Also listen to the Miles Davis take.)
Theme tune of "The Flintstones."

Note: This is a very important jam-session favorite and must be memorized.

6.22
THE MINOR I AND THE DESCENDING HARMONY

If a minor chord is not part of the II-V-I progression and the melody note is not the minor 7th, it can usually be re-harmonized as a minor/Major7 or a minor 6 chord.

If the minor I chord can be played over more than one bar, then this chord can be re-harmonised using the minor/Major7 and minor 6 creating a harmony that falls down chromatically. Look at these four chords in the key of Cminor.

Cm	CmΔ7	Cm7	Cm6

The highest note of the first chord is C.
Of the Cm/Maj7 it is the note B.
On Cm7 it is B♭.
And lastly on Cm6 it is A.
C – B – B♭ – A (*a chromatic line – descending*)

One can imitate this chromatic movement in the bass using slash chords creating a descending bass line.

Cm	CmΔ7/B	Cm7/B♭	Cm6/A

These above chords are actually the first four bars of the tune, "My Funny Valentine."
You can also use this progression over two bars as in the tune, "In a Sentimental Mood."
Here it actually happens twice starting on Dm then on Gm. Even though it is not written as a slash chord, the bass player can play the descending chromatic bass line.

Dm DmΔ7	Dm7 Dm6	Gm GmΔ7	Gm7 / Gm6 A7

<u>Now for the improvisation.</u>
First, be aware of and use the chord tones and any other note you hear. But if we look at the chords academically, this is what we derive:

Cm	CmΔ7	Cm7	Cm6
C Dorian	C Melodic minor	C Dorian-----------------------------	

Notice that the Melodic minor and Dorian scales only differ in one note – the 7th.

Dorian: C–D–E♭–F–G–A–(B♭)–C

Melodic min: C–D–E♭–F–G–A–(B)–C

Try this progression on any tune that has a few bars of the I minor chord. For example "Summertime," which starts with 4 bars of Am.

6.23
PEDAL NOTES

A bass note that is played at the bottom of the harmony over a series of different chords without changing the pitch of the bass note, is called a PEDAL NOTE or PEDAL POINT. Pedal notes create slash chord harmony that creates tension and release in the music.

A good example is John Coltrane's tune "Naima," a complex beautiful composition that makes use of many interesting slash chord and pedal note harmonies. Here are the chords:

"Naima"

D♭Δ7/E♭	E♭m9	AΔ7/E♭ GΔ7/E♭	A♭Δ7
D♭Δ7/E♭	E♭m9	AΔ7/E♭ GΔ7/E♭	A♭Δ7
BΔ7/B♭	B♭13(♭9)	BΔ7/B♭	B♭13(♭9)
DΔ7#5/E♭	BΔ7/B♭	A♭Δ7/B♭	E♭sus/B♭

Pedaling is great way of starting or ending a tune. Experiment by pedaling on the 5th note of the tonic key. For example, if the tune is in C major, the bass player should pedal the note G.

6.24a
GIANT STEPS

If you are interested in playing jazz, then studying John Coltrane's tune from 1959 called "Giant Steps" is a must. This tune is a good example of the special chordal system that Coltrane derived at and is sometimes referred to as the "Coltrane Matrix", a system of building on the key centres that are a major 3rd away from one another. This is a jazz jam session favorite, so memorize this tune.

Here are the changes for "Giant Steps"

BΔ7 D7	GΔ7 B♭7	E♭Δ7	Am7 D7
GΔ7 B♭7	E♭Δ7 F#7	BΔ7	Fm7 B♭7
E♭Δ7	Am7 D7	GΔ7	C#m7 F#7
BΔ7	Fm7 B♭7	E♭Δ7	C#m7 F#7

Playing walking bass lines and improvising over these changes can be a little awkward at first because of the unusual key centre movement and the fast tempo, (one crotchet = +/- 286 bpm).

<u>Here is a brief analogy</u>
An augment triad is built up in intervals of major 3rd's, i.e. B augmented = B–D#-G, and divides the octave into three equal parts. Moving backwards on the augmented triad (B-G-D#), Coltrane built a Major7 chord on each of these notes, BΔ7 to GΔ7 to E♭Δ7. See the diagrams below. In the first 3 bars, the Major7 key centres happen at the beginning of every bar, from BΔ7 to GΔ7 to E♭Δ7, and then similarly from bar 5, GΔ7 to E♭Δ7 to BΔ7, it goes down in Major 3rds. From bar 9 (the second half) he changes direction and moves up in 3rds on every 2nd bar.
He then completed the composition by adding V7's and II–V's before the Major7 key centres.

```
    [-----3rd down-----][----3rd down------]
```
BΔ7 D7	**GΔ7** B♭7	**E♭Δ7**	Am7 D7
--(I) V7-----------I	V7-----------I		II---------V7-----------

```
    [----3rd down------][----3rd down------]
```
GΔ7 B♭7	**E♭Δ7** F#7	**BΔ7**	Fm7 B♭7
--I V7-----------I	V7-----------I		II---------V7----------

```
    [------------------3rd up-------------------][-----------------3rd up--------------------]
```
E♭Δ7	Am7 D7	**GΔ7**	C#m7 F#7
--I	II---------V7-----------I		II----------V7----------

```
    --][-------------------3rd up--------------------]
```
BΔ7	Fm7 B♭7	**E♭Δ7**	C#m7 F#7
--I	II---------V7-----------I	(Fine) II---------V7----------	

6.24b
THE COLTRANE MATRIX

Question: how do we re-harmonize a II-V-I progression using the Coltrane Matrix?

Answer: Using the key of C as an example,
Step 1:
write out the II-V-I progression

Dm7	G7	CΔ7	/ / / /
II	V	I	

Step 2:
With C augmented in mind, re-harmonize the progression by working back from the tonic chord CΔ7 in the fourth bar. If we go up a major 3rds we get EΔ7, then up another major 3rd we get A♭Δ7.

Dm7	A♭Δ7	EΔ7	CΔ7

Step 3:
Fill in all the V7's that lead to the major7 chords.
i.e. V7 of A♭Δ7 is E♭7
    V7 of EΔ7 is B7
    V7 of CΔ7 is G7

THE COLTRANE RE-HARMONIZATION OF THE II-V-I

```
  II------------------------------------------------------------V------------I
| Dm7      E♭7    | A♭Δ7      B7    | EΔ7      G7    | CΔ7                    |
      V-------------I      V-----------I      V------------I
```

A good example is Coltrane's re-harmonization of the Miles Davis piece "Tune Up," resulting in the Coltrane composition called "Countdown."

6.25
'TWO CHORD' PROGRESSIONS

We've done the Blues in its various forms, The II-V-I, the Turnaround, Rhythm Changes, the Descending Minor I and The Coltrane Matrix progressions. However. there are a few other smaller progressions that one needs to understand. I will just touch on a few of them with small examples, no explanations, just improv ideas under the chords, so you can experiment using your ears.

THE REPEATED CHROMATIC CHORD PROGRESSION

With only two chords a semi-tone away from one another, these "two-chord" progressions can be extremely challenging so don't under estimate them. The aim is to make the improv horizontal (melodic) and not vertical.

Example 1: "Night in Tunisia" (First 6 bars)

E♭7	Dm6

E♭ Lydian Dominant D Dorian

Example 2: "The Girl from Ipanema" (intro)

F∆7	G♭7(♭5)

F Lydian G♭ Lydian Dominant

Example 3: "Caravan" (First 12 bars)

C7	D♭7

Option 1: C Blues --

Option 2: C Altered------------- D♭ Altered------------

Option 3: C Phrygian#3 ------------------------------------

Option 4: C Blues---------------- E♭ Major triad-------

Example 4: "Well You Needn't" (First 6 bars of the A section)

F6	G♭6

Option 1: F Major pentatonic G♭ Major pentatonic

Option 2: G Major triad-------- A♭ Major triad------

I TO IV WHERE BOTH CHORDS ARE DOMINANT
A familiar rock jam session favourite.

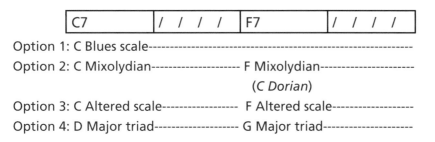

C7	/ / / /	F7	/ / / /

Option 1: C Blues scale--

Option 2: C Mixolydian-------------------- F Mixolydian--------------------

                               (C Dorian)

Option 3: C Altered scale------------------ F Altered scale------------------

Option 4: D Major triad-------------------- G Major triad--------------------

CONCLUSION

CONCLUSION

Studying and discovering the secrets of music is an endless and exciting journey. This book is a small part of that journey and once you have studied the jazz theory section, you should be able to work out and understand western scale/harmony theory that I have not covered here. When you have learnt the basics, you must learn to discover and work things out for yourself.

INTERVALLIC PERMUTATIONS

Scales should first be memorized and practised in a conventional way, i.e. "up and down", "down and up", etc. When you can play the scales in an even legato-feel at, say, a metronome marking of four, 16th notes = one click = 80 bpm, (Aim to play four 16th = one click = 120 bpm, so that you can handle different musical situations), you should then practice them in a more musical way using diatonic intervallic permutations, 3rds, 4ths, 5ths and so on. Diatonic meaning the notes that belong to that scale. For example, going up the scale in 3rds would mean making use of major as well as minor 3rds, but when we use the word diatonic, it is not necessary to write the word major and minor. Apply these four permutations formats to all your scales.

> 1. Ascending
> 2. Descending
> 3. Alternating ascending – descending
> 4. Alternating descending – ascending

Here are examples using the C major scale. Note: when going up the scale ascending, stay ascending going down. Similarly, when going up the scale descending, stay descending going down. This way one is able to create a non-stop loop, which is good when practising them.

Here is an example using intervallic thirds:

1. Ascending

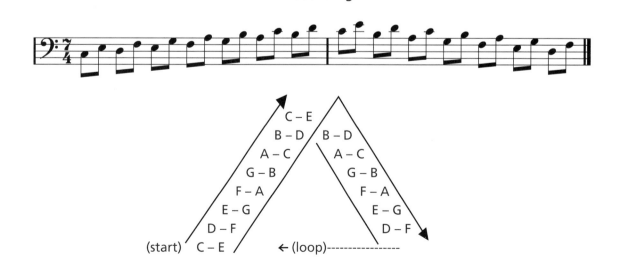

2. Descending:

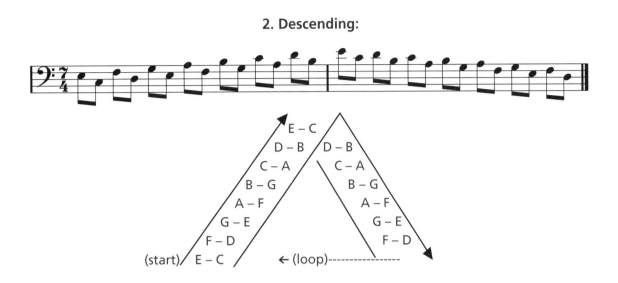

3. Alternating ascending – descending:

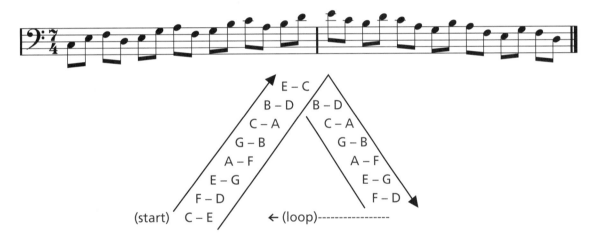

4. Alternating descending – ascending:

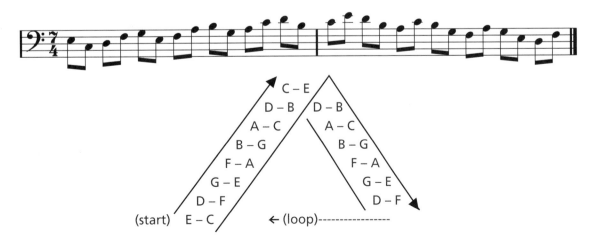

IMPROVISATION

My own conviction, from performing and teaching, is that every person knows how to improvise and frequently does, the most common everyday improvisation being conversation. When people talk, especially in their mother tongue, they improvise with words that come naturally, creating flowing phrases. However, at the beginning these words were not natural, they were learnt through constant repetition until they became part of our vocabulary and we developed. The more literature we read, the more sophisticated our conversation became. The same is true with performance, improvisation and ultimately, composition. The musician uses what comes naturally, with the music embedded in the subconscious.

A SHORT TIP ON LEARNING TO IMPROVISE

Internalize these scales, develop good time, tone and technique, study harmony, then put on your favorite CDs, forget everything in this book and listen for the notes as you jam along. YOU MUST DEVELOP YOUR EAR TO HEAR THE NOTES, even if you don't know what chord is being played. Remember that you are always only a semi-tone away from the correct note, so don't be afraid to jam. FEAR (AS WELL AS EGO) IS CREATIVITY'S WORST ENEMY. Listen and hear what you play, and in time you will begin to play what you hear. Then, you will listen hard to the harmony and try to sing the melody in your head: Don't play the scales but play what you hear and feel. Make music from your heart and not your head. The spirit of music is more important than the mathematics of music.

ARTISTRY AND ORIGINALITY

I would like to end this book with what I feel is the most important aspect of music. My interest in the artistry of music as opposed to technical procedures has had a profound influence on how I compose and play music. I have spent years trying to understand the relationship between music and artistry, so that I may not only become a more original musician, but so that I may also understand how to lead and inspire other musicians, to bring the best out of them and take my music (and theirs) to a higher level in performance and story-telling.

Stephen Nachmanovitch writes in his book, *Free Play: Improvisations in Life and Art,* "The creative process is a spiritual path. This adventure is about us, about the deep self, the composer in all of us, about originality, meaning not that which is all new, but that which is fully and originally ourselves" (1990, 13).

"Fully and originally ourselves", to me, means a sound that is authentic, honest and expresses one's personality, feelings and voice. It does not need to be a huge innovation along the lines of Schoenberg , Miles Davis or Jaco Pastorius. Some of what I have done may have been done before, but not with my voice: my tone, dynamics and ideas. We are not all innovators but we ARE all originals with a totally unique DNA blueprint, and therefore do not need to stand in the shadows of the great masters. When you were a child you were not scared to be yourself, therefore learn from this book, but more important, try to find and play from your inner child, the one that is originally you.

Enjoy the journey,
Carlo

BIBLIOGRAPHY

DiBartolo, Joel. 1997. *Serious Electric Bass*. Florida: Warner Brothers Publishing.

Haerle, Dan. 1975. *Scales for Jazz Improvisation*. Indiana: Studio P/R, Inc.

Levin, Mark. 1995. *The Jazz Theory Book*. Pentaluma: Sher Music Co.

Nachmanovitch, Stephen. 1990. *Free Play: Improvisations in Life and Art*. New York: Penguin Putnam Inc.

Ricker, Ramon. 1976. *Pentatonic Scales for Jazz Improvisations*. Florida; Columbia Pictures.

Suggested reading and studying:

Adolfo, Antonio. 1993. *Brazilian Music Workshop*. Advance Music, Rottenburg.

Bailey, Derek. 1993. *Improvisation: Its Nature and Practice in Music*. New York: Da Capo Press.

Bellson, Louis. 1985. *Modern Reading Text in 4/4*. Alfred Publishing Co., Inc.

Cage, John. 1968. *Silence*. Marion Boyars Publishing, London.

Del Puerto, Carlos. 1994. *The True Cuban Bass*. Sher Music Co. Pentaluma.

Goldsby, John. 2002. *The Jazz Book: Technique and Tradition*. San Francisco: Backbeat Books.

Hal, Crook. 2006. *Beyond Time and Changes – a musicians guide to free jazz improvisation*. Advance Music, Rottenburg.

Khan, Hazrat Inyat. 1996. *The Mysticism of Sound and Music*. Boston and London: Shambhala Publications.

Levin, Mark. 1995. *The Jazz Theory Book*. Pentaluma: Sher Music Co.

Mariano, Charlie. 2000. *An Introduction to South Indian Music*. Advance Music, Rottenburg.

Nachmanovitch, Stephen. 1990. *Free Play: Improvisations in Life and Art*. New York: Penguin Putnam Inc.

Reid, Rufus. 1974. *The Evolving Bassist*. Warner Brothers Publishing, Florida.

Taylor, Eric. 2006. *The AB Guide to Music Theory, Part 1*. The Associated Board of the Royal Schools of Music. London.

Werner, Kenny. 1996. *Effortless Mastery: Liberating the Master Musician Within*. New Albany: Jamey Aebersold Jazz, Inc.

VHS Video Tape: (not available on DVD)
Prestia, Francis Rocco. 1993. *Fingerstyle Funk*. International Music Publications Ltd, Essex.

ABOUT THE AUTHOR

Photo by Raymond Romke.

Self-taught bassist/composer Carlo Mombelli was born in Pretoria, South Africa. After studying classical piano for six years he started playing bass at the age of sixteen and seven years later one of South Africa's most important jazz guitarists, the late Johnny Fourie, asked him to join his band together with Duke Makasi on saxophone and Kevin Gibson on drums. The group had a contract at a club in Johannesburg to perform jazz six nights a week for six months. This was Carlo's school of music. In 1985 Carlo started the group Abstractions, developing and performing his original compositions at weekly gigs in downtown Johannesburg clubs. They recorded for Shifty records.

Carlo has since recorded and performed at many festivals around the world from Brazil to Europe, including the Rome Villa Celimontana International Jazz Festival, the Stockholm Jazz Festival, the Moers Festival, the Leipziger Jazztage and Jazz an der Donau festivals in Germany, the Paris Banlieues Bleues festival, and the open air Rio Loco festival in Toulouse France, the Cape Town International Jazz Festival, and the open air Festival Mundial in Holland – with amongst others, Egberto Gismonti, Lee Konitz, Mick Goodrick, Charlie Mariano, Peter O'Mara, Frode Nymo, Häkon Mjäset Johansen, Wolfgang Haffner, Jeroen Van Vliet, Adrian Mears, Bill Elgart, Raiz de Pedra, Barbara Dennerlein, Samuel Blaser, Simone Soul, Dejan Terzic, Tutty Moreno, Francois Jeanneau, Carine Bonnefoy and the Ethel String Quartet.

Carlo also contributed music and played on the 1989 tribute for Jaco Pastorius, "Basstorius," which also features bassists Mathew Garrison, Carles Benavent and Dave LaRue.

Besides his original music, jazz and Brazilian music gigs, he has also played many other styles, from salsa with Connexion Latina with Daniel Moreno and Anthony Martinez, folk music with Shawn Phillips, blues with USA blues legend Louisiana Red, pop music with Gloria Gaynor and Johnny

Logan, to concerts with the popular German "liedermacher", Konstantin Wecker.

Back home in South Africa he has worked with some of the best, amongst others, Barney Rachabane, Khaya Mahlangu, Kesivan Naidoo, Lulu Gontsana, Ian Herman, Gito Baloi, Bheki Khosa, Louis Mhlanga, Vusi Khumalo, Themba Mkhize, Afrika Mkhize, Mark Fransman, Bruce Cassidy, Waddy "Ninja" Jones (*Die Antwoord*), Andile Yenana, Sydney Mnisi, McCoy Mrubata, Tutu Puoane and Siya Makuzeni. He can also be heard as a bassist on many South African recordings including, amongst others, with Tony Cox, Johnny Fourie, Tlale Makhene, Zim Ngqawana, Marcus Wyatt, Simphiwe Dana, Sibongile Khumalo and Miriam Makeba.

In addition to the many ballets that have been choreographed to his music, with performances around the world, from Johannesburg to Amsterdam, Denmark and the Ramallah Dance festival, he has also composed music for more than 14 films, documentaries and animations (winning an award at the Hiaff Animation festival in Tokyo 2005), which have been shown at all the major art film festivals from New York's Museum of Modern Art (MOMA), to Berlin, London, Toronto and the Sundance Film festival.

His composition commissions include, amongst others, *Observations From the Hideout* , commissioned by the Swedish "Stockholm Saxophone Quartet" to new works for Piano and Wind ensemble commissioned by SAMRO, the South African Music Rights Organisation, that also commissioned Mombelli to compose music for the voice finalist at the SAMRO Endowment's Overseas Scholarships competition. In 2004 he also composed and conducted music for Zim Ngqawana's 50-piece orchestral performance.

Carlo Mombelli has also recorded several CDs and DVDs of his own works and performs his music with his ensembles Abstractions, The Prisoners of Strange and Mombelli's Trance by Chance. He has been nominated three times for a SAMA (South African Music Awards) for his recordings, *When Serious Babies Dance* (2002), *I Stared into my Head* (2007) and *Theory* (2010), which also features cover artwork by Norman Catherine and Kay Hassan.

From 2007 to 2009, Jean-Louis Mechali, a composer, musician and director of the Paris-based company, "Lutherie Urbaine", employed Carlo to conduct weekly workshops in Soweto and Mamelodi teaching children to play his music on instruments built from recycled material. Carlo also worked with this company for many weeks in Paris. The result was a series of concerts in South Africa and France with the children, Carlo and musicians from Paris. The filmmaker, Sylvie Coulon, documented the project in a film called *Sharp Sharp*.

Carlo has been featured in many books and magazines including, *Classicfeel*, the American magazine – *Bassplayer*, the French magazines – *So Jazz*, *Impro Jazz* and *The Jazzman*, the German magazines, – *The Bass Professor*, *The Jazz Zeitung*, *The Stereo*, *Day In Day Out* Music Magazine, and the German *Jazz Podium*, and the books *Soweto Blues* by Gwen Ansell, and *In Township Tonight* by Dr. David Coplan

In the 90s, Mombelli worked as an orchestral copyist for the G Ricordi & Co. Publishers, copying with a calligraphy pen, Hubert Stuppner's *Concert Musique KV91 Amadeus* for flute, clarinet and string orchestra; Martin Kalleyn's *Miniatur Eins*; Rolf Ruhm's *Berceuse* for a 104-piece orchestra and Gerhard Stäbler's *Co-wie Kobalt* for solo contrabass and an 88-piece orchestra.

Besides performing, composing and recording, Carlo has been involved in music education for many years. In 1998 and 1999 he held a teaching post at the Richard-Strauss Conservatoire in Munich, Germany, and in Johannesburg where he resides, he was Composer-In-Residence at Wits University in 2004. In 2006 he was the musical director for the Standard Bank National Youth Band

and took this handpicked group of the best South African young music students for a one-week trip to the Stockholm Conservatory in Sweden.

In April 2010 he was Artist-in-Residence at the Birds Eye jazz club in Basel, Switzerland, where he worked and gave composition and performance workshops with students from the Basel Jazz Academy. In the same year he was invited and did a bass master class and performance of his works at the Berklee College of Music in Boston, USA and the Swiss Bern Jazz School.

Carlo currently holds a teaching post at The University of the Witwatersrand (Wits), Johannesburg, where he received a doctorate in composition (DMus) in 2009.

www.carlomombelli.com

 Carlo uses DR Handmade Strings on all his instruments

SELECTED DISCOGRAPHY

1. Abstractions – On The Other Side (Shifty Records 1986)
2. Carlo Mombelli – Abstractions (ITM Westwind 1988)
3. Carlo Mombelli and Charlie Mariano – Happy Sad (ITM Pacific 1992)
4. Basstorius – The Marathon Runner (Hotwire Records 1993)
5. Martin Kälberer – Espaco (KCM Verlag 1994)
6. Raiz de Pedra and Egberto Gismonti – Diario de Bordo (Enja Records 1996)
7. Carlo Mombelli – Dancing in a Museum (ITM Pacific 1996)
8. Carlo Mombelli and the Prisoners of Strange – Bats in the Belfry (Baobab Art Records 1997)
9. Zollsound 4 with Lee Konitz – Open Hearts (Enja Records 1998)
10. Marcus Wyatt – Gatherings (Sheersound 2000)
11. Tony Cox – China (Instinct Africaine 2002)
12. Zollsound Chamber Ensemble – Songs Closer to Silence (Enja Records 2002)
13. Johnny Fourie – Solo, Duet & Trio (Instinct Africaine 2002)
14. Tlale Makhena – The Ascension of the Enlightened (Gallo Records 2004)
15. Nibs van der Spuy & Barry van Zyl with Shawn Phillips – Hadeda (Rhythm Records 2004)
16. Carlo Mombelli and the Prisoners of Strange – When Serious Babies Dance (Instinct Africaine 2004)
17. Simphiwe Dana – Zandisile (Gallo Records 2004)
18. Miriam Makeba – Makeba Forever (Gallo Records 2006)
19. Marcus Wyatt – Language 12 (Language 12 records 2007)
20. Carlo Mombelli and the Prisoners of Strange – I Stared Into My Head (Instinct Africaine 2007)
21. Carlo Mombelli and the Prisoners of Strange – Live at Fort West, 2004, DVD (Melt 2007)
22. Marcus Wyatt – Language 12, Live at the House of Nsako, DVD (Language 12 Records 2009)
23. Carlo Mombelli – Abstractions Retrospective – 86 to 92 (2009)
24. Carlo Mombelli and the Prisoners of Strange – Theory (Instinct Africaine 2010)
25. Live at the Bird's Eye Jazz Club, Compilation, Volume 11 (Roche'n Jazz 2010)